COOKING
ON THE LINE

from Food Lover to Professional Line Cook

By Wayne Cohen

Quote from p. 209 from "Medium Raw" by Anthony Bourdain
Copyright © 2010 by Anthony Bourdain. Reprinted by
permission of HarperCollins Publishers

Larousse Churchill Publishing Corp.
Chicago, Illinois 60657

Printed in the United States of America

ISBN: 1453778195
ISBN-13: 9781453778197
LCCN: 2010912647

Cover photograph from left to right:
Miguel Solorio, Wayne Cohen, and Chef Tony Priolo

To my wife Andy,

Whose support and love helped make this fantastic adventure happen.

This is a true story.

Some of the names in this book have been changed.

*"As far as cuisine is concerned one must read everything,
try everything, see everything, observe everything,
in order to retain, in the end, just a little bit!"*

-Chef Fernand Point, *Ma Gastronomie*

PROLOGUE

The alarm goes off. I bang the snooze button and roll over. No reason to jump out of bed today. Everything's covered at the restaurant – the new guy, whom I've been training all week, should be well into completing today's prep. And thankfully it's my last lunch shift. I know my station like the proverbial back of my hand – so I sleep a little longer.

When I finally climb out of bed, I wander over to the window and look out. It's supposed to be late spring. But one glance at the bare trees lining the streets, bending in the frigid lake winds, tells me it's still the dead of winter. I take my time getting ready for work. No reason to hurry. Nothing to worry about.

I drive to the restaurant at a leisurely pace. The streets are still busy with morning rush hour traffic, but I'm not stressing about a thing. I'm a professional, and I know exactly how long it will take me to be ready for service today.

Arriving at the restaurant – which is situated on a busy street corner in the heart of the city – I park and go inside. As I enter the kitchen door, the succulent aroma of a long-reducing veal stock greets me. I slowly go down the back stairs to the basement prep area, and hear the blasting salsa music on top of the banter and laughter.

"Buenos Dias, everybody!" I loudly announce as I hit the bottom of the stairs and gaze into the fluorescent-lit tiled chamber of stainless steel prep tables and walk-in cooler and pantries. The four morning cooks and their helpers are busily chopping, mixing, butchering, and making pasta at their respective stations. "Buenos Dias, Amigo!" comes the chorus of replies.

I turn the corner, moving past the pasta guy, and I hear some more friendly greetings: "Good morning, Senor! Buenos Dias, My brother!"

Reaching my locker, I put on the uniform: herringbone chef pants, black clogs, and embroidered chef coat, which I calmly button up. I grab my knife bag, and I go back up to the kitchen.

As I approach my station – Grill-Sautee – the chef looks up from his work and gives me one of his steely glances. "Did you tell the guy to come in late today?"

"No, Chef," I reply. "Absolutely not."

"Well he's not here."

The briefest pause here. We both know what this means – what a no-call no-show necessitates in a top professional kitchen at a fine restaurant.

It's go-time for me.

One more time.

• • •

Now I'm moving like my ass is on fire. Back down the stairs to the prep area. Back to the walk-in cooler. Time is ticking.

I start grabbing ingredients for today's service: basil, rosemary, sage, arugula, spinach, broccolini, potatoes, capers, cannellini beans, garlic, eggs, parmesan cheese, tomatoes, olives, chick pea flour, Italian sea salt, onions, bread crumbs, spring mix, fish stock, veal stock, and wild mushrooms…

…and I stop for a moment. *Surprised? Why should I be surprised?*

But there's no time to philosophize about such things. I have sixty minutes to knock out three hours worth of prep before the day's first meal is served. I know I'll get it done. This is what I do.

When I get back to my station I check my low-boy coolers. The Meat drawer: Veal Scaloppini, Pork Medallions, double chicken breasts. Next in the seafood drawer: Shrimp, Calamari, Octopus, Salmon, Mediterranean Sea Bass filets – all there.

Next I check the squirt bottles: Caper sauce, House Vinaigrette, Lemon Juice, Lemon oil, Marsala wine, Extra Virgin Olive Oil, White wine – check!

I turn to my fresh herbs and I'm madly chopping when the chef comes over.

"What fish do we have for today's special?" he asks.

"Branzino," I tell him.

"How do you want to do it?"

"Asparagus and roasted rosemary potatoes," I suggest. "With a citrus caper sauce."

"Sounds great," he says, and quickly goes back to the myriad tasks facing *him* that day.

I quickly glance at my watch – twenty minutes and counting, I spin around to the grill - load the wood and charcoal and get it fired up - I'm back to my prepping and can now feel the heat from the flames on the back of my neck.

I'll get it all done. Quickly. Precisely. Deliciously. Because I'm a professional line cook, but I wasn't always…

PART ONE

INTO THE FIRE

"There is no lying in the kitchen. And no God there, either. He couldn't help you anyway. You either can or can't make an omelet. You either can or can't chop an onion, shake a pan, keep up with other cooks, replicate again and again, perfectly, the dishes that need to be done. No credential, no amount of bullshit, no well formed sentences or pleas for mercy will change the basic facts. The kitchen is the last meritocracy, a world of absolutes; one knows at the end of each day how one did."

-Chef David Chang
Medium Raw
by Anthony Bourdain

1

CHAPTER 1

TWO YEARS EARLIER...

I t's a quiet summer day on the northwest side of Chicago, and I'm sitting in my office, on my computer, scrolling down the employment opportunities in the local food, beverage and hospitality industry, when I see a simple headline. At that point I am completely unaware that I'm staring my future in the face:

HARD WORKING LINE COOK NEEDED

There's an old saying that luck happens when preparation meets opportunity. I know all about that. I've always been an extremely proactive person – on the fast-track, career-wise. At the age of twenty-five I was executive vice president of a software company that eventually went public. A couple of years later I started my own business – a services firm for the computer industry, which eventually morphed into a systems company.

Then, lo and behold, I had the opportunity to be the president of an international cookie manufacturing company. In fact, I thought I would be a cookie guy for the rest of my life. But then, events beyond my control started to change the dynamic at the company. What had been a lot of fun at first – and very successful – was turning out to be somewhat less than a laugh riot.

All of which is why, on that fateful summer day – the moment I lay eyes on that want-ad in "Craig's List" – I wonder if it's the opportunity I've been looking for: the doorway into a world I've been thinking about entering for a long time:

HARD WORKING LINE COOK NEEDED

I scroll down the job description:

> Searching for someone who possesses the ability to take pride in hard work, has a passion for simple food, and can execute to the finest level. The restaurant will be opening in two weeks, small kitchen, work directly with the chef. Great opportunity for culinary students or recent graduates. Without a doubt a fun and knowledgeable environment. Focus is on German Cuisine, eventually the best in Chicago. Please reply without delay.

I'll be the first to confess that I'm not even remotely a recent graduate of some fancy culinary school. But that's kind of the point of this whole adventure, which will become clear soon enough. At the bottom of the job listing it says I can reach a person named "Dan" – who I later learn is the chef – anytime after 8:00 am. There's a phone number and an email address, and I'm looking at my watch and thinking, *why not?*

"Hello, this is Dan," the man himself answers after a couple of rings.

"Hi, my name's Wayne Cohen, and I'm calling about the ad on Craig's List, the one for the line-cook job?"

"Right, great, so…" There's a slight pause, and I know what's coming next. "…what kind of experience do you have?"

I nod to myself, prepared for this question. "Okay, well, the truth is, I haven't been in the restaurant industry for many years. But I was when I was younger."

I explain that I worked in restaurants as a kid, but over the last several years I've been a successful businessman, and am currently in the process of selling my interest in my company. But what I *don't* tell him is that I'm all of fifty-two years old, and have been trying to deal with this strange transition period now for a while, waiting for my buy-out deal to solidify. I've never been one for complacency, and I've always wondered, as far back as high school: Should I have pursued the culinary arts as a career?

Maybe it's an absurd notion. Anyone can have a passion for food. Your mom might adore your meatballs more than life itself. Your Uncle Ernie might be *gah-gah* for your goulash. But going from the ooh's and ah's of quaint dinner parties at home to parties of eight, all night long, working the line, in the trenches of a real restaurant kitchen, serving hundreds of discerning diners, night after night? That's another kettle of fish altogether. I'm well aware of the odds, but the odds don't matter. I have to try. In fact, for the first time in my life, I have the *option* to try.

So I start seriously looking for just the right opportunity – and Dan's place seems perfect. It's close to home. I would be working directly with the chef. It's a start-up environment rather than an established routine. And its culinary focus is on German cuisine, which I've always enjoyed and, at this point, seems somewhat unique to me.

After listening to me explain my background, the guy named Dan says, "Okay. Fair enough. So what's your familiarity with food?"

"I have a passion for food," I tell him. "I cook all the time and I'm always reading about it."

"That's good."

"And I have pretty decent knife skills." Now I'm hoping I don't sound too... *what*? Eager? Naïve? "Although I'm sure they could get a lot better."

"Okay."

"I can sharpen my own knives."

"Good."

"That's about it."

Without skipping a beat, the voice says, "Fine, come on in tomorrow at nine in the morning." He gives me the address, and that's that.

The journey begins.

Chicago, among many other things, is a food town. The tradition dates back to the early nineteenth century, when the city was the primary connection for transporting livestock from the wild-west to the rest of the country. Chicago's Union Stock Yards became "hog butcher to the world" and Chicago became the city of Big Shoulders. Throughout the next century and a half, the melting pot of nationalities and immigrant palates created one of the most interesting and vibrant restaurant scenes on the planet. Today, world-class chefs like Grant Achatz, Rick Bayless, Charlie Trotter, Art Smith, and Graham Elliot Bowles, all call Chicago home.

This new German restaurant – the one at which I would be interviewing – is located in a densely populated area, a neighborhood which I know very well. Not far from my home, Lincoln Park is a teeming labyrinth of *nouveau riche*, college students, and yuppies, north of the city. The area bristles with upscale boutiques, bookstores, restaurants, theaters and trendy coffee shops. The German place – we'll call it the Hofbrau – is situated near the "El" (elevated train), on a block crammed with storefronts.

The night before my interview, I discuss the whole situation with my wife. I want to be sure she knows the ins and outs of a restaurant schedule: late nights, weekends, maybe being on call.

"Listen, Wayne, I know it's something you feel passionate about," she finally says, looking at me across the dinner table that night with the kind of expression a teacher gives a student who wants to take a crack at solving the theory of relativity. "I say go for it."

At that point, I give my wonderful, understanding, patient wife a big smile. "Great, because I've got an interview tomorrow morning at 9:00 am."

She chuckles. She knows me well. She always tells people, 'Whenever Wayne starts a sentence with "I love…" it always has food on the end.' She also knows, all too well, that I'm not exactly an early riser – hell, I'm not even forming complete sentences before 11:00 a.m. So the notion of me getting up at the crack of dawn – and having to be "on" for an interview – is extremely humorous to my beloved life partner.

My wife Andy is a petite, fit woman with an open, friendly face and a quick smile. I, on the other hand, am built like a Brinks truck, bulked up from a lifetime of working out, as well as the physical discipline learned from my years of playing college football and competitive weight-lifting. Little do I know, at this point in my adventure, that my size and stamina would come into play soon enough in the crucible of the professional kitchen.

That night, I manage to get to bed at a decent hour, and I get up the next morning chomping at the bit.

I look through my closet, wondering what I should wear to my interview. Technically this is the first formal interview I've had since… well, since the stone age… so I'm a little out of practice. Should I go the sport coat routine? No, that seems a little much. Maybe sport coat and jeans? Nah. I'm thinking no jacket. I finally decide on a nice pair of slacks and a blue dress shirt, something in that middle range of casual/professional.

It's a beautiful, warm July day, and I give myself enough time to get to the restaurant early. The sky is a brilliant blue over the busy streets of Lincoln Park, and I'm feeling good. I find the restaurant – a modest little storefront with a new sign out front – and I go inside.

The place is a construction zone. Contractors are working, there's sawdust everywhere. It's loud. There's a sense of chaos in the air. But despite the mess, I can already see the interior design taking shape, and it looks authentic to me – or at least how I would imagine a German beer hall would look at Oktoberfest. Dark brick flooring and long wooden tables. The Black Forest chandeliers. *Nice Concept,* I think. *Somebody's actually got some brains here.*

I walk up to one of the construction guys. "Excuse me, do you know if the chef is here?"

He points across the room and he says, "Go talk to that guy."

I turn my head and I see who he's pointing at, and I'm a little taken aback. He's in his early thirties – maybe – and he's wearing cargo shorts, a t-shirt, a baseball cap and glasses. Not exactly the tony look one would expect for big time restaurant management. I approach him. "Excuse me, are you the chef?"

"No," he says, "but who do you represent?"

Who do I represent? The question catches me off-guard. He must think I'm a salesman. Or maybe he thinks I'm an inspector from the City. "My name's Wayne Cohen, and I'm here for the cook's job."

He looks me up and down. He's really checking me out now, trying to get a bead on me. Of course, at that point, it doesn't occur to me that I'm old enough to be his dad.

So I decide to ask: "And who are you?"

"I'm the owner," he says.

"Oh, great, it's good to meet you," I say, shaking his hand. "Wayne Cohen."

He introduces himself, and he says, "Look, the chef's not here yet, so why don't you go have a seat over there."

"Okay, great."

I side-step the workman and I go sit down at a corner table, and I wait.

And wait.

Ten minutes pass. Fifteen minutes. And finally the owner comes over and says, "The chef's usually here by now, but he hasn't shown up yet. You want to take off, and maybe come back later, or maybe call?"

Now I'm thinking he's trying to get rid of me. I think about it for a second. The sound of a nail gun pops in the background. A drill screams. Something tells me to stay put. I've been working up to this for years. I'm not going to bail out now – giving up at the first sign of inconvenience.

So I tell the young owner: "No, it's alright, I took off the whole morning for this, so I'll just wait awhile – if it's okay."

He looks at me once again like I just told him I'm a visitor from the planet Krypton.

"Suit yourself," he says, and turns and walks away.

Looking back on it, I can tell you one thing that kept me glued to that bench, waiting and waiting for the chef to show up, watching the workman futz with the wiring: *curiosity.* I've always been curious to know what it would be like to be one of those guys in the white jackets doing their magic behind the looking glass of a restaurant kitchen.

The fact is, I've always loved to cook. Even when I was a kid, growing up in Skokie, Illinois, a leafy, near-north suburb where deli's outnumber the fine dining establishments. I began cooking in grade school. I would cook things when my parents went out – omelets, toasted cheese sandwiches with mustard and lettuce, and real French fries instead of those gnarly baked lunch-lady fries – which, of course, delighted my sister. At age thirteen I got a phony work permit and got a job at McDonalds. And I eventually got to work the grill, which I loved. At fifteen I got a gig in a rib and chicken joint and learned how to do things like make barbecue sauce, season and fry chicken, and make biscuits. Every summer my dad would make me the grill man for outdoor barbecues – making Italian sausages in an exotic marinade of Wish Bone dressing, and of course, my specialty, the patty melt.

But the truth is, throughout my childhood, cooking was always just an enjoyable diversion, a pleasant way to earn pocket money. It was better than working at a gas station – which

I had done – but it was only the beginning of what would become a grand passion.

The fact is, food did not become a serious obsession until I was an adult.

People who are serious cooks know who they are. We're the people who read *Cook's Illustrated*, *Food and Wine*, *Bon Appetite*, and *Saveur*. We're the ones who have a library of cookbooks, including well-thumbed editions of *Larousse Gastronomique*, Julia Child's *Mastering the Art of French Cooking*, and *Beard on Food*. We're the ones for whom every meal is the most important event of the day. We're constantly reading restaurant reviews and the food section of the newspaper, clipping recipes, and going that extra mile to find that perfect ingredient. And when we go out to eat, we're the ones who will drive two hours out of our way to find a great meal. Generally speaking, we are obsessed with reading about, experimenting with, thinking about, and eating food.

Years ago I even toyed with the idea of opening my own restaurant. I had gotten to be a pretty damn-good home cook. I would make killer rib roasts with various sauces. I would sauté a fantastic veal piccata. I would make these delicious Gratin Dauphinois potatoes, which are wafer-thin slices of russets baked in cream until they get golden brown and taste just heavenly. I would also make a Bolognese sauce that would just knock people over – slow simmered, with milk, white wine, and nutmeg, and a splash of cream at the end, which would just send it through the stratosphere.

My dinner guests would often remark, "You know so much about food. You'd be a great chef." And at times I would even play around with potential names for my own place. I'd come up with sample menus, and concepts, the whole shot. My friends kept saying, "You should! – You should! You should totally open your own place." People say this to each other all the time, but nobody really knows what opening a restaurant truly entails – the brutal hours, the personnel headaches, the relentless competition, the financial risk, all the odds stacked against you. Being a pretty shrewd businessman, I would usually say to my pals, "Thanks, but the truth is, I don't want to blow my own money on it." And they would sometimes even say, "We'll back you." But I would always just smile and thank them for the kind thought.

The problem is, I'm a pragmatist. Even back then, I knew owning a restaurant was a lot more than just walking around, glad-handing people and kibitzing and being the impresario like Humphrey Bogart in *Casablanca*. Especially in Chicago, which has become such a foodie town, and the home to so many star chefs. I had come to know some of these chefs. These are men whom I admire and respect – true masters in their chosen field, with years and years of experience. These are my influences.

Which is probably why – when Chef Dan finally appears that day at the Hofbrau – I am once again a little perplexed by his youthful appearance.

He walks in dressed in the same slacker-casual motif as the owner – camo shorts, t-shirt, gym shoes. He's a big, stocky young guy, and he can't be a day over twenty-eight. He's got one of those Abe Lincoln beards, and he looks like he just either chopped down a tree or finished playing with a grunge band. And here I am in my natty Italian slacks and dress-collar shirt, feeling more like a chaperone than the next big gun in the restaurant industry.

This big, strapping kid walks up to me and introduces himself: "Hi, I'm the chef, Dan."

I have to admit, I like this guy immediately. I can't really explain it. He has a kind of friendly, open manner on top of this layer of confidence – maybe it's just quiet professionalism. Or maybe it's the sports thing. A serious wrestler in high school, Chef Dan grew up looking over the shoulder of a German mother, who was a great cook. After high school, he went to culinary school and worked for some of the city's finest chefs.

I'm shaking his hand now. "Wayne Cohen, Chef. Nice to meet you."

We sit down and we start talking food; and I elaborate on what I told him on the phone. I tell him about my passion for cooking. I tell him that I've been to some great restaurants, both here and in Europe, and that I know good food when I taste it. And then I look at him and say, "And I eat a lot."

He gets a huge kick out of this. He laughs, and then he asks me if I eat a lot of German food.

I give him a nod. "I like it a lot, I've cooked it, and I've been to Germany." Then, with a shrug I confess: "I wouldn't profess to be an expert on it."

"Yeah, well," he kind of smirks at this, "not too many people are."

He goes on to explain that his concept for the place is to have a scratch kitchen – in other words, everything made in-house. He wants to feature an excellent, well-executed menu, and he eventually wants the place to become the best German Restaurant in Chicago.

For some reason, at this point, it doesn't sound like a delusion of grandeur to me. Maybe it's the young chef's confidence. Or maybe it's the lack of truly good German restaurants in Chicago and surrounding areas. This was not always the case. By the end of the Nineteen Century, there was a German ale house – known as a *bierstube* – practically on every other street corner on the north side, churning out the sausages and Weiner Schnitzel. Over the next hundred years, nearly a quarter million Germans flowed into the metro area. The Chicago/Milwaukee corridor came to be known as the "German Athens," and Chicago became home for a number of rustic German drinking and dining establishments.

But today, among the major contenders, whose cuisine is the best? It's debatable.

I'm thinking it's an honorable goal.

"Tell me a little more about your experience," the chef finally asks.

I launch into my tale of childhood fast food joints, and ribs and fried chicken and biscuits, and working as an apprentice chef at a country club during high school. The fact is, I actually flirted with the idea of cooking as a career back then. But then football came into my life and changed everything.

It was back when I was in junior high, I found I was good at something other than dropping French Fries into hot oil, and that was *running into people*. I was a small, skinny kid, but I had this knack for drilling kids twice my size. I started playing in the Pop Warner leagues in seventh grade, and I loved it. By the time I was a freshman at Niles North High School – still only five-foot-one and a hundred and thirteen pounds – I was the smallest kid on the 'A' squad. But in no time I became starting middle-linebacker, and was named captain by the first game. Sophomore year they almost brought me up to varsity, and I kicked butt for the next three years, kicked enough butt that I was recruited by several Division-1 schools – including Drake University – at a mere five-foot-five, a hundred and seventy-two pounds.

A year later I'm sitting on the bench at Drake, and learning to hate the whole program, when I decide to transfer to the University of Toronto. When I arrive at the U. of T. a year later, I've grown three inches and gained about forty pounds of muscle. I started playing for the Varsity Blues immediately as a starting linebacker. I played in every game throughout the rest of my tenure at Toronto, I made a lot of great friends, and I graduated. I knew I was never going to go pro – I was too short – but I was probably shaped into the person I am today by football – driven, confident, disciplined, physical.

Of course, I don't go into the whole football thing with Chef Dan on that sweltering July day with the workman banging away in the background. Mostly what we talk about is food, which, by this point in my life, has become my favorite subject. And we talk for nearly an hour that day. An hour is a long time for a busy chef in the throes of opening a new place. I take it as a good sign.

He shows me the menu, and it really sinks a hook into me. Aside from the usual suspects – the customary Spaetzle, schnitzel, sausage and sauerkraut variations – I'm seeing some true gastronomic *chutzpah* here. I'm seeing some twists on the classics that show a nimble mind and a willingness to invent. Take the beer-braised mussels with bacon, for instance. Or the Roasted Smoked Pork Chops with the Honey-Butter Braised Savoy Cabbage; or the Almond-crusted Chicken Schnitzel; or the Braised Duck with a Red Cabbage Pretzel Bread Pudding. I'm seeing all these unique takes on old standards and I'm getting more and more excited.

One entry that really speaks to Chef Dan's creativity is the Skirt-steak Rouladen with Roasted Fingerlings in a Red Wine Sauce. Rouladen – which comes from the French word *rouler*, or "to roll" – is a European dish usually made by wrapping a thin slice of meat around a filling, and then braising it until it's tender and succulent. The German version is traditionally made with top round or a piece of chuck, but Chef Dan's variation gives the dish a beefier, bigger flavor. The skirt steak comes from the bottom (or belly) of the cow, and it can be tough if over-done, but a correct cooking method can really bring out the best in this flavorful cut of beef.

And speaking of bellies, another item on the menu that catches my eye is the Pork Belly Reuben. I know Reubens. I've been eating and enjoying them all my life, but this is something altogether different. Pork belly is basically uncured, unsliced bacon, found low on the hog, which requires a long cooking time. I have a passing familiarity with the cut, but I'm looking at the menu and I'm thinking this sounds delicious: Braised Berkshire pork, sauerkraut, and Caraway Havarti cheese, all on grilled rye bread. This menu is actually making me hungry. Again, a good sign.

We talk some more, and eventually I wrap up my part of the conversation by saying, "Anyhow… I understand you're in a start-up situation, and I'll be a really dependable person for you."

He nods appreciatively, and then he looks at me with a kind of anticipatory expression on his face, as though he's about to broach an essential subject. "What are you looking for as far as pay?"

I give him a deferential shrug. "I understand this is an internship position, and I'm actually okay with not getting paid."

Again, he does not skip a beat. "No, you're going to get nine dollars an hour."

The slightest pause here, as I look at him, wondering if I've actually just gotten hired for the first time as a professional cook without even noticing it.

Finally, almost without thinking, I give him a single word response: *"Sweet."*

CHAPTER 2

Knives. One does not fool around with one's knife. I discover this early on in my journeys – the knife is the central tool of the craft. The knife for the professional cook is like the pool stick for the professional pool hustler. Usually cloistered away in a lined case or leather roll-bag, a cook's cutlery is a reflection of their personality, their pride in their work, their mastery. For years, I have used Henckels' knives at home, a very popular brand manufactured in Germany, which I plan to bring along with me to the Hofbrau. And by the time I embark on this quest to become a working line cook, I have pretty good skills. I can do the slice and dice at a pretty fair clip. But – as I am about to learn – I still have a lot to learn.

But before I do that, I have to learn something else – knife skills notwithstanding – and that is whether or not I am actually being *hired*. At the end of that first interview, Chef Dan was a little vague about the plan: "We'll be opening in a couple of days," he says. "I'll give you a call on Sunday to check in."

After the interview I bop out of the place feeling like a million bucks, but as the days pass, a strange kind of ambivalence sets in. Did he actually say he was going to hire me?

Or did he say he was only *considering* hiring me?

By Sunday I haven't heard a thing, and I'm still wondering if I imagined the whole thing or if I'm actually going to be a cook. So I figure I'll be a little more aggressive — I'll do what I do in business: I'll call him and put it to him directly.

He answers the phone on the third ring, and he rants for a few minutes about all the delays: the electrical taking too long, the contractors running behind. At last he says, "It's going to be a few more days until we open. I'll give you a call and let you know soon."

"Sorry to hear about all the delays," I say.

"Whattya gonna do? That's the biz."

"Can I ask you a question?"

"Of course."

"When you finally open up, I'm just wondering, are you going to hire me?"

Again, without missing a beat, he says, "Absolutely. You can be part-time if you want, but I absolutely want you to work with me."

This time I'm definitely keeping my elation to myself, but I'm thinking: *Sssswwwweeeeeet.*

•   •   •

I often think in football metaphors. I can't help it. I'm a product of the gridiron, and once you get football in your blood, it never leaves you. If you look at a professional kitchen as a football team, the chef is like the coach, or in some cases, the coach *and* the owner. The *sous chef* is the quarterback, executing plays, and the line cooks are the players running the plays. In the days leading up to the Hofbrau opening, I'm ready to run any play Chef Dan chooses to call.

The week after that glorious Sunday, Dan and I talk again, and he tells me to come in on a Thursday to help him set up the kitchen.

Thursday arrives and I show up at the restaurant to discover the place is really coming along. The fixtures are all in, and the room really looks like an authentic German beer hall.

I find Chef Dan in the Hofbrau kitchen. It's a blazing hot, narrow affair – very small – closed off from the dining area by a narrow hallway. As you enter, the first things you see are multi-level counters of stainless steel, facing you, where finished dishes are placed. This is also known in restaurant parlance as the "pass." The back wall of the kitchen has the line of cook stations – the fryer, the six burners, and the flat top grill – underneath which lay the twin ovens, which keep the place up near a hundred degrees most of the time. Flanking the right side of the grill is the steel prep table. Directly across from the cooking surfaces are low-boy reach-in refrigerators, topped with a long narrow cutting board running its length, as well as the "speed table," which hold metal containers, in graduated sizes, to be filled with the day's ingredients. Past the speed table and low-boys are the dishwashing station, the walk-in cooler for the beer kegs, the freezer, and the reach-in cooler.

I'm looking at this kitchen and thinking it's not a lot of room for a place the size of the Hofbrau. Much less than I had expected. But then again, I don't know what to expect.

Dan turns to me and says, "I need to go down to the knife store. Why don't you come with me?"

"Great, how do you want to get there?"

He shrugs. "We'll take the 'El.'"

"I got a car," I say, and it was as though I had just said I own my own commercial airliner.

"Great," he says with a shimmer of admiration in his eyes. "You drive."

We hop in my car and we head downtown. On route, Dan talks about what he wants to do with the restaurant. We discuss the menu, the opening date, and the staff. I mention the Berkshire Pork Belly Reuben again, and Chef Dan tells me how it's prepared. He tells me how you season the bellies with salt, pepper and dry mustard, and then braise them – fully submerged in water, with onions, carrots, celery, garlic cloves, and tomatoes* – in a 325-degree oven for five hours.

---

* three each; onions, carrots, celery, garlic cloves, (all rough chopped), and 1 cup of crushed tomatoes, 2 tablespoons of spicy mustard can substitute 1 tablespoon of dry mustard, 1 tablespoon kosher salt and 2 teaspoons black pepper. Cook in a covered pot or roasting pan covered with aluminum foil.

When it's done, you shred it and keep it ready for orders. To make the sandwich, you put the reduced braising liquid in a hot pan and add the shredded pork to warm it up. While the meat is warming, you butter two pieces of rye bread and grill them on the flattop, then you hit each piece with a thick slice of caraway havarti cheese. Then you top one of the bread-slices with the Riesling-braised sauerkraut, and when the belly is hot and juicy, you drop a healthy portion of that on top of the kraut. The other slice of rye – which is now enrobed with melted and oozing Havarti – goes on top of the belly. Finally you cut diagonally and *voila!* You're on the express train to heaven. Spicy mustard or whipped horseradish strictly optional.

Hearing Dan describe this – with all the pride of a fine craftsman describing the mosaic of a cathedral ceiling – I'm getting so hungry again I'm practically drooling.

In fact, even at this early stage, it's becoming clear to me that what Chef Dan has in mind for the Hofbrau is a German version of what has come to be known as a Gastropub. First made popular in England in the early 1990s, the name is a combination of pub and gastronomy, and usually refers to a bar that specializes in high-qualify food. Gastropub menus are many notches above the standard pub grub you find at most taverns, but still offered in the casual atmosphere of a watering hole. They are the Anglo equivalent of the French *brasserie*.

In fact, ironically, in early Twentieth Century Germany, the original Hofbrau houses served fine food in a beer hall environment. This is the *plan* for Chef Dan's place.

But I'm about to learn that the restaurant business is a series of sliced and diced plans.

We arrive at the knife store, and we pick up Chef Dan's new equipment, and I get my first knife bag. I'm really feeling like I'm in the thick of it now. And tomorrow I'll be prepping for service.

The next morning I come in dressed for kitchen work. Earlier that week Dan had suggested I wear chef pants – which I did not own at the time – or as an alternative I could wear cargo pants. I picked up a new pair of cargo pants, so now I'm decked out proper. Chef Dan provides me with the requisite white jacket and apron to complete the universal uniform.

The upcoming weekend has a big neighborhood street fair roaring into Lincoln Park. And although the restaurant isn't quite ready to serve a full-menu, the owners – and Dan – think it would be wise to create a limited menu for the festival. The idea is to get some buzz going, not to mention some much needed cash.

So I walk in that morning, and I look at the owner and Chef Dan, and I'm kind of taken aback. They're disheveled, stressed out, ragged. Dan looks as though he hasn't slept in weeks. There seems to be an uncertainty hanging over the place – a question of whether we're going to, in fact, open before the weekend. In the kitchen I gently ask him what the deal is, exactly when we're going to pull the trigger on the place.

"We're discussing that right now," he says. "The owner still hasn't made up his mind."

"He's being kind of wishy-washy, isn't he?" I comment, not thinking much of it. Little do I know this wise-crack is going to come back and bite me very soon.

"Yeah, well... anyway," Dan says with a shrug, "first thing I'm going to need you to do is go and grab twenty onions and julienne them. Alright?"

"Yes, Chef."

In the military hierarchy of a professional kitchen, the word chef is both rank and term of respect. You learn to respond to commands accordingly. "Yes, Chef," is the appropriate reply to any request. "Yes, Chef, I will chop that parsley." "Yes, Chef, I will swab that deck." "Yes, Chef, I am your bitch."

But now I'm thinking, this is it, I'm really going to be cooking. My first task. Cutting onions. And the beauty of it is this: we are starting with nothing. We are building a menu from the ground up. This is what cooking is all about. So I'm really pumped up to do great job on these damn onions. I'm going to show these youngsters what I can do.

Basically the process of julienning onions is simple: With a sharp knife you chop the ends off the onions, and cut them in half, stem to root. Then you peel them and slice them to a one-eighth-inch thickness for sautéing purposes. The menu at the Hofbrau uses onions extensively – especially as accompaniment for all the different sausages, which is what we would be serving at the street fair.

So I grab the first onion, and then I pick up one of the house knives, grasping it firmly by the handle, and I'm using the standard pinch grip with my finger near the heel – and the heels on these things are very sharp – and I immediately realize something is wrong.

I've cut myself.

Oh crap.

It's not a bad cut, just a nick, but I look down at the pearl of blood forming on my finger and I'm thinking: My first task, and before I even have a chance to slice a single vegetable, I've cut myself.

"Don't worry about it," Chef Dan says, coming over and handing me a Band-Aid.

"Sorry, Chef." I sheepishly apply the Band-Aid to the nick.

"Don't sweat it," he says. "It's good luck."

"Good luck?"

"Yeah, it's a tradition. When you're opening a restaurant, somebody gets cut, it's good luck."

This is the kind of guy Chef Dan turns out to be: Positive, encouraging, friendly, hard-working. From that moment, he was always right there in the trenches. If I'm working on twenty onions, he's always right next to me working on twenty of something else. The more I get to know this guy, the more I like him.

I continue julienning the onions. I'm slicing the halves, and then I'm slicing the thinner sections, and I'm feeling good. I get one done and I show the julienne slices to Dan. "Is this right, Chef?"

"Looks good."

Now I'm on a roll, prepping ingredients, most of which will fill the speed racks. These ingredients form what is known among cooks as the *mise en place* (mise ehn plahz) – a French term, literally meaning "putting in place." The contents of the speed racks form the essence of every station. Celebrity chef Anthony Bourdain thinks of his "mise" as a religion – a sort of hallmark of the professional cook's preparedness – and that's not too far from the truth. All the components are measured out, washed, sliced, diced, chopped, minced, roasted, pureed, liquefied, emulsified, or prepared in myriad other ways in anticipation of the day's requirements.

Taken together, the ingredients begin to define the essence of a cuisine itself, and I will soon learn the staples of the Hofbrau "*mise*" required to prepare Chef Dan's creations:

♦ Bacon Dressing in a Squirt Bottle
♦ Lemon Yogurt Dressing in a Squirt Bottle
♦ Roasted Shallot Sherry Vinaigrette in a Squirt Bottle
♦ Pomace Oil in a Squirt Bottle
♦ Roast Garlic
♦ Cucumbers
♦ Grilled Onions
♦ Lardons (diced bacon)
♦ Chopped Shallots
♦ Chopped Garlic
♦ Chopped Parsley
♦ Dumplings

- Crispy Leeks
- Crispy Red Onions
- Poached Eggs
- Carrot Tomato Slaw
- Red Cabbage Bread Pudding
- Red Wine Mushroom Cream Sauce
- Honey Butter-Braised Savoy Cabbage
- Potato Pancakes
- Tempura Beer Batter
- Braised Sauerkraut
- Honey Mustard
- Dijon Mustard
- Apple, plums
- Apple Butter
- Applesauce
- Candied Lemon Peel
- Roasted Fingerling Potatoes
- Red wine
- Butter
- Kosher Salt and pepper
- Beer Braise
- Reduced Pork Belly Braise

The contents of a *mise en place* can vary wildly from restaurant to restaurant – from cuisine to cuisine – but the *mise* itself is absolutely paramount to a well-run restaurant kitchen. It is the artist's palette – the culinary color wheel. As my friend, mentor, and future boss, Chef Tony Priolo, has often remarked, "If you don't have your "*mise*" right, you will never be a success in this business."

But on that sweltering Friday at the Hofbrau, I'm just starting the process, and around the eighth or ninth onion, I make a couple of observations.

First of all, remarkably, the onions are not making me cry. I can't explain it. Other people are walking in – the owner, workmen – and it's something like ninety-eight degrees in the kitchen. I have a thermometer in my jacket pocket most of the time, and I would occasionally pull it out and just hold it up in the air. Most of the time it would be up around the century mark. And now the onion fumes are wafting as well, and people are marveling that I'm not crying.

I may be bleeding, but damn it, at least I'm not crying.

Second of all, my wrist is getting tired, and I'm thinking my mandolin at home would be really nice right about now. A mandolin is a rectangular kitchen gadget designed to slice uniformly and thinly, and it makes julienning a breeze. But I'm also thinking that, although Dan is young, maybe his technique is old-school. Maybe he wants to do everything by hand, and I can respect that. So I just grab another one and julienne away.

I do the twenty onions. I show the results to Dan. "Is this okay, Chef? Is this what you had in mind?"

He's happy with my work, and he gives me my next task: Dice thirty shallots. Dicing shallots is like working with pygmy-sized onions, very tedious, very time-consuming. But

I'm getting into it. I'm finding my rhythm, and I'm cooking in a professional kitchen, and I'm learning more and more with each task.

Chef Dan insists that I write down whatever I learn – he's very particular about this – so I'm keeping copious notes. After the shallots are done, the chef orders me to make a custard for the red cabbage pretzel bread pudding.

So I pull out my note-pad:

> Classic custard = separate 12 egg yolks, whip the yolks with 1 qt of cream

Next he asks me to make some mayonnaise from scratch: so I pull out the eggs, separate the yolks, get the oil, the sherry vinegar, the Dijon mustard, and the salt, and I start whipping it up by hand. I catch myself thinking wistfully about my Cuisinart sitting on my kitchen-counter at home.

The chef keeps giving me tasks to complete, and I am looking around the kitchen for supplies and ingredients. But the reality is, we're in a small kitchen in a restaurant that has a big menu. He and I are grabbing items, moving them, setting them down again. We're not in the best kind of flow, so everything is more hectic than it ought to be.

I turn my attention to meat.

Dan butchers meat by eye – another example of that old world German mojo – and he can hack off a series of perfect six-ounce portions without batting an eye or having to weigh anything.

My job is to pound the portions of beef into submission until they're no thicker than a quarter of an inch – eventually to be breaded for Jager Schnitzel, topped with a red wine, mushroom cream sauce. I use a tenderizer, which is a gadget with a bunch of nail-like prongs to break the tissue down, and then I use a meat pounder. So I tenderize the first piece and then I start slamming the hell out of the thing with the pounder.

And nothing's happening. The meat is going nowhere. And I'm hitting it, and I'm hitting it, and I'm thinking: Where did this stuff come from? So finally, I pause, sweating from the effort, and I go over to the reach-in cooler to read the label on the package (to see what kind of cut and grade I'm dealing with here). Sure enough, it's top sirloin – and it's USDA Choice, too – which boggles my mind.

I can't believe how hard I'm pounding on this stuff. I have pounded less strenuously on running backs with quicker results. My back is starting to hurt. Finally, mercifully, the meat does flatten, and I get the things pounded out, and I'm off to the next task, feeling a strange kind of epiphany brewing within me.

I decide to forget about my appliances at home making things easier, and I decide to let all the second-guessing go. I decide to just go with the flow. I'm thinking: I'm just the cook. I'll just do what the chef wants. Period. And this is a key moment for me – a moment that will pay off with dividends very soon.

In fact, at that point, the only trace of doubt that still lingers in my mind has to do with something that I have been wondering about for a long time – something far more serious than a cut here and there – something that could easily put the kibosh on my budding career.

During the previous autumn, I started experiencing excruciating lower back pain, and associated sciatic nerve pain. I went to see a chiropractor and he told me to stop lifting weights. He showed me the problem on x-rays. He explained that I have degenerative spine issues, including compressed discs and bone spurs, which may be causing the sciatic pain. And he tells me if I don't take it easy I may very well end up in a wheel chair. At that point, I'm not taking this news very well. He finally says, "If you don't believe me, go see an orthopedic surgeon."

I did. And the surgeon sends me for an MRI after taking more X-Rays. He then tells me that my back isn't as bad as the chiropractor said, but I still have lots of issues, including Spinal Stenosis – narrowing of the spinal cord, which is pinching and playing havoc with my sciatic nerves, so I do need to take it easy. Meanwhile I'm seeing a second chiropractor, and he has me on a regimen of stretching therapy and special exercises, which not only seem to be completely useless and ineffective, but also seem to be exacerbating the problem. I'm not a happy camper.

And I'm wondering: Am I paying the piper for a lifetime of weight-training and hard-hitting sports?

Finally a third chiropractor gets me on a program of adjustments and acupuncture, which, miracle of miracles, start to make me feel better. I stick to the routine for months, but the progress and pain relief is slow, painfully slow. Eventually

I go back to the surgeon for a follow up consultation after a second MRI. About a week before I embark on my cooking adventures, I find myself back in the surgeon's office, listening to his prognosis. "It's like I thought," he says with a shrug. "You've got degeneration, you've got arthritis, you have Spinal Stenosis, and you have a 2mm nerve sheath tumor in your spinal cord."

"So what do I do?"

"You just… live with it. We will monitor the tumor annually. You keep working out, keep doing your yoga. You can lift. You just listen to your body and use common sense."

This is good enough for me.

But now, on this balmy July afternoon, in the crucible of the Hofbrau kitchen, I'm plunging into this very physical world of professional line cooking, standing all day, reaching, twisting, moving fast and furious in tight quarters, and pounding the crap out of sirloin chunks. And I'm wondering: Physically, am I in good enough shape to pull this off? I haven't stood on my feet for ten hours a day since I was a kid in high school.

Despite my back pain, though, I am completely determined. Despite getting up early, despite standing all day, despite being the senior citizen in a restaurant kitchen full of twenty-somethings, despite everything: I am going to do this. I am going to do whatever it takes.

Which is exactly what I find myself doing that first day. We're working side-by-side, Chef Dan and I, and we're rocking and rolling, prepping everything for service. Sure, we're just beginning with a limited menu, but soon we'll be moving up to full-service, and we need to be ready. So I'm being a good employee, a team player, and doing what I'm told.

At some point that day, I leave the kitchen area to grab a glass of water, and the owner comes around the corner, and he walks up to me and says: "Look, I'm not wishy-washy."

This totally catches me by surprise. I realize, almost instantly, that he heard the comment that I made earlier that day to Dan about whether or not they're going to open their doors. *This guy's got good ears*, I'm thinking, *I'll give him that.* "I'm really sorry," I start to say, "I shouldn't have –"

"Look," he says, cutting me off. "I'm just not sure if we can open right now."

This is getting more awkward by the second. I nod sympathetically and say: "You're the boss, I apologize for making the comment. There's no need to explain your decisions to me."

"But I just want you to know," he says, looking at me with this intense kind of expression. "I really want to open, but I just want to do it right."

"You're the boss," I say with a nod, and go back to my business in the kitchen, thinking, *This relationship is going to be interesting.*

In the restaurant business, a new place works up to its grand opening in stages. Very often, the owners will quietly open their doors in the days leading up to a grand opening in hopes of getting some walk-in business without any formal advertising or announcements. Known in the industry as a "soft opening," the idea is to generate word-of-mouth, and also give the staff and kitchen a chance to get their game on and work out the kinks.

Dan and the owners decide to go ahead and open softly that Friday night — taking advantage of the foot traffic, and gearing up for the street festival the next day — and though we're working on a limited menu, there is much to do. And I also realize I'm actually cooking for the public now, which is a new experience for me, and I like it. Even though I'm still primarily prepping ingredients, and I'm closed off from the front-of-the-house action, it's still a subtle adrenaline charge.

Meanwhile Dan is churning out the plates for the walk-in traffic. The plan is for the Hofbrau to eventually include a lavish assortment of Wursten (sausage), which will feature Bratwurst (seared or poached), Veal Bratwurst (seared or poached), Thuringer (smoked pork, seared), Knackinger Asch (firm pork, cold or poached), Bockwurst (veal, pork, and chives, poached), and Landjager (air-dried pork, jerky-style).

I continue to be impressed by Dan's ambition and taste and creativity. But at one point, between sausages, he asks me to make German Eggs (also known as Scotch eggs). For the reader who has not had the dubious pleasure of a Scotch egg, the basic idea is this: take a hardboiled egg, wrap it in pork, bread it in flour, egg, and pretzel crumbs, and then deep fry it.

On the single occasion that I had forced one of these puppies down my gullet (somewhere along the line), I found it very reminiscent of well-seasoned cardboard. But it's the job at hand, so I hard-boil and peel 12 eggs. After discussing the gentle art of boiling eggs, it's time to season and taste the pork. And this is the one time I manage to upset my chef.

An interesting thing about Dan: He is a terrific guy, but he has a pretty short fuse. Throughout my tenure as his line cook, I generally manage to stay on his good side, but that first day, the German egg turns out to be a minor little bump in the road.

The idea is to season the pork with dry mustard and salt. I usually season things pretty heavily with salt, so that day I go ahead and season the pork, and we cook a piece of it, and we taste it, and the chef says to me: "It needs more salt." So I season it again (and put in a lot of salt). I cook another piece, and he gives it a taste. Again he says, "Needs more salt."

So I'm working on the third one, and while I'm seasoning the ground pork, he's grumbling: "This is the third try, and there better not be a fourth."

I nod and take this in – realizing I've just witnessed the limits of Chef Dan's patience – and I'm fine with that. Some chefs have hair-trigger tempers. Professional kitchens, as I am about to learn, seem to breed human behavior in the extreme. But Dan is not a screamer or an egomaniac whiner or a manipulator; he's simply a perfectionist – as are all great chefs. So I salt the heck out of the pork. And finally it flies.

I spend the rest of that night quietly doing what I'm told, and enjoying the simplicity of the job at hand. I roast peeled garlic cloves in olive oil at 450 degrees, which is a terrific way to create not only a bunch of savory roasted garlic, but also a fragrant, delicious flavored-oil. I also roast some oxtails for a traditional oxtail soup. The process of roasting bones for a stock is a professional kitchen essential – similar to the creation of the ever-popular veal *demi glace* – and it's one of the reasons restaurant food often blows away home cooking in depth of taste.

I put in eight hours that day – eight straight hours in a blistering-hot kitchen on a sultry summer day – and to be completely truthful, the time actually flies by. I'm having a ball, and it's not until I come back the next day, which is a Saturday – the first day of the street fair – that I truly realize exactly why I'm having so much fun at a job that is so physically demanding.

Saturday arrives. The big Lincoln Park Street Fair. I come in and the prep is a little more involved now, the full *mise en place* taking shape, the menu coming to fruition.

The interesting thing about working in a restaurant kitchen is that there aren't many measuring tools, and you have to get used to working with large quantities of ingredients. As a home cook, you go out and buy your foodstuffs, and then you go home, meticulously measure everything, cook, and then eat, enjoying the fruits of your labors. It's over in minutes, and it's time to clean up. When you're working as a professional line cook, however, you are doing this repetitively. And you're rarely eating anything. You're prepping and then you're cooking, and cooking, and cooking, and cooking, and cooking. Over and over and over. It begins to hone your skills and instinct. You begin to just *know* when things are right – by sight, smell, and taste. You begin to build up confidence.

That day, right off the bat, I peel and grate twelve potatoes and make potato pancakes. Then Dan shows me how to trim some pork loin. I use my own knife at first, the Henckels from home, and then Dan suggests I try his knife. I'm amazed at the improved feel and sharpness of the thing – my first encounter with a Japanese-made Shun, which becomes my knife-of-choice from then on – and pretty soon I'm commenting to Dan, "Man, this knife is *something*, I could make Carpaccio with this thing."

Next I pound veal, chicken breasts, pork, and skirt steak for schnitzels and Rouladen. I roast duck and sauté *mirepoix* – the holy trinity of diced aromatic vegetables: onions, carrots, and celery – and then I deglaze the pan with red wine and braise the duck.

And all of it eventually leads me to the epiphany.

I'm standing there at the prep table, chopping like crazy, and it hits me. I'm actually enjoying this on a level I've never known before. I'm enjoying the simple *act* of this simple, repetitive work. Sure, I love food. And yeah, I'm proud to be working as a professional cook all of a sudden (without embarrassing myself too much). But something happens to me then on a deeper level.

You can call it the "zen" of professional cooking, if you want. The word itself comes from the Japanese pronunciation of the

Chinese word *chan*, which means *quiet*. The Sanskrit root of the Chinese word also means "to see, to look at," and that's actually what I start doing in the Hofbrau kitchen. I'm simply doing my duties, one at a time, quietly, meditatively, seeing each task clearly, and enjoying it to the point where the work becomes almost therapeutic.

There's something so calming about dealing with a simple task. Focusing on one thing at a time. Just being in the present moment. I'm an hourly employee, I get paid the same for an hour regardless of what I am doing... so I just do what the chef wants, one task at a time, one hour at a time.

It all washes over you, and the strangest thing happens: the stress begins to melt away.

Unfortunately, on that muggy July Saturday, I am completely oblivious to all the unexpected events – and people – that are about to threaten my new-found inner peace and enlightenment.

CHAPTER 3

Controlled chaos. Taming the Tornado. The Pressure Cooker. Choose your favorite metaphor – the professional restaurant kitchen is everything you've heard and more. But aside from the heat, the exertion, the relentless multi-tasking – at its core, the restaurant kitchen is all about the team. The legendary French Chef Escoffier, back in the 1900s, developed a "brigade" system for the professional kitchen – resulting in an almost military hierarchy – that continues to be the industry standard even today. But somehow this system seems to have fallen through the cracks at the Hofbrau.

This is something I notice over those early days: The dynamic here is virtually void of any hierarchy. The way people address each other here – regardless of seniority or rank – is stunningly cavalier. The dishwashers respond to the general manager as if they're talking to another dishwasher. The wait staff addresses the chef as though they're addressing the dishwasher. Very soon, it seems to me, the owner will be getting very little respect from virtually anybody he employs. I cannot quite figure it out. Is it a generational thing? Is it that slacker sense of entitlement? Is it unique to this place, the whole industry? Does everybody think they're empowered nowadays?

That first weekend, I'm observing all this while we get slammed by foot traffic from Lincoln-Fest. And we're not really ready for that kind of action. The Hofbrau does not even have the beer taps in yet. They have to rig these bogus portable taps that look like big Igloo coolers out in the front to accommodate all the patrons. And this is a *German beer hall* we're talking about here. And even though we're basically just serving sausage sandwiches, pretzels, and German eggs that first weekend, it's a surge of orders we haven't truly prepared for. And Dan wants to have the whole menu up and running by Monday. So I'm extremely busy, generally keeping to myself, not being very social, not saying much to the rest of the staff. I figure it's best to just focus on my skills. But I'm getting to know people simply by observing.

For the most part, the rogue's gallery of staffers at the beginning of my tenure, with whom I will be working on a daily basis at the Hofbrau, are good, hard-working people – with a few exceptions. Over the course of the next few weeks, I develop a sort of battlefield camaraderie with many of them. Some are already on their way out. The owner – we'll call him Tom Rothman – I've already encountered with my awkward "wishy-washy" comment, and we're not saying very much to each other at this point. Which is probably for the best.

The general manager – another late twenty-something, usually clad in that trademark slacker garb of cargo shorts, sneakers and t-shirts – is a guy named Adam. General Managers in the restaurant business are supposed to do just that – generally manage – which includes hiring and firing, scheduling, and so on. I find out Adam is fond of wearing black bandanas and is usually doing shots of Rumplemintz by noon each day. And if there's one thing a restaurant does *not* need it's a drunk general manager.

The wait staff includes a wisecracking young gal named Jody, who, I find out very soon, is Chef Dan's sister. This will lead to some interesting dynamics. Working in tandem with Jody is a gal named Nina. She's a lovely person. Very nice. Unfortunately she is the worse server I have ever seen. In the coming weeks, even the customers will begin to comment that Nina's a disaster. I will secretly come to think of her as Nina The Scourge of All Restaurants.

Joining me in the kitchen as a fellow cook is a young lady named Allison. A serious but friendly sort with a lot of experience, Allison is also currently working as a line cook at a restaurant called The Fiddlehead Café (like many cooks, she has a second job). My wife, always one to find the humor in my nightly war stories, starts calling Allison "Fiddlesticks" – and the name sticks.

We have three dishwashers at the outset – Pedro, Albert, and Terry. Pedro is a compact little Columbian fellow, raised in the U.S., barely five-foot-four in heels. He's a good worker and wants to go to culinary school. Albert is a big, heavy-set black kid with big round glasses, very chatty and in-your-face, with a family at home to support on minimum wage. Terry is a little older, rail thin and boyish, habitually drifting off into his own little world.

Watching Terry, noticing the little tics and noises he makes, I begin to wonder if Terry doesn't have some sort of mild disability. I never find out for sure, but he's a likable enough kid. A loud *"Yes sir!"* is Terry's standard retort to any negative comment directed his way.

In addition to the staff running around, bumping into each other, there's also still a retinue of workman hanging around that first weekend, trying to get the place up to speed for Monday's opening. For the most part I'm able to ignore them. But at one point on Saturday, as I'm prepping, and Dan is somewhere else, this carpenter comes through the kitchen, screaming, "Did anybody see my ladder?!"

He's really wound up, and I just respond with my customary silence.

He yells some more, bellowing in this tiny kitchen: "I said: Did anybody see my goddamn ladder?!"

I continue to calmly mind my own business – happy in my zen-like state.

He approaches me and looks at me like he's looking at a wad of gum on his shoe. "Don't you understand English?"

I just look at him.

He raises his voice even higher. "Do you understand what I'm saying to you?!"

At that point, I calmly say, "I don't know where the fuck your ladder is. Do you understand that?"

The guy looks stunned, then he turns and bolts out of the kitchen like it's a fire drill, and I hear Albert the dishwasher behind me, howling with laughter.

It's probably the first thing this kid has ever heard coming out of my mouth. He comes over and grins at me, his eyes twinkling behind those coke bottle glasses. "Whoa! Whoa! I knew you had somethin' going on there, man! Oh yeah! I knew you was quiet but you was thinking a lot!"

I just smile and shrug. Maybe he thinks I'm a hard ass now. Maybe that's a good thing. I don't know.

We each go back to our respective stations, and before long, we're getting so busy that Chef Dan comes in and asks me to help with the pretzel and sausage sandwich production. The orders are coming fast and furious now. And I learn how to plate the stuff – you put this here and that there – and we're knocking them out. We're using those little paper "boats" and everything is moving quickly now and I realize once again, I'm really doing it. I'm cooking for the public now.

The whistle has blown, game on, and I'm running plays down the field.

The first week passes in a blur of special events, mini-crises, delays, small victories, and false starts. Before opening, we have a couple of Grand Tasting events: the first one for a group of invited guests – some of Dan's friends, other chefs and cooks, tattooed, hipster foodie types – and a second tasting for the staff. The idea is to have a sort of culinary dress rehearsal, allowing everyone to taste the whole extensive menu, which is pretty incredible: The mussels braised in beer with bacon, onions, garlic, and butter; the beautifully crafted potato pancakes; the various schnitzels with the different sauces; the skirt steak Rouladen; a thick smoked pork chop called Kassler, with cabbage braised in sherry vinegar, butter and honey, served with a pan sauce of plums and apple over the top. I act as a server for the first tasting, which is a new experience for me, and I find myself taking pride in the level of food we're working with here.

All of the dishes are top notch. Except for one: a radish yogurt soup.

This soup may be the only misstep in an otherwise amazing spread. One of Chef Dan's friends claims it's one of the worst things he's ever tasted in his life. When I hear this, I can't help but be amused. Even Michael Jordan hits an air-ball once in a while.

The desserts – another one of Chef Dan's blind spots – don't quite live up to the entrees: a lemon poppy seed muffin (brought in from a local bakery) with a homemade yogurt whipped cream; a dessert Spaetzle (deep-fried frozen Spaetzle on ice-cream, dusted in cinnamon); and orange granita, which is kind of an upscale snow cone made with fancy flavors and ice (served with a shot of Goldschlager, which is a cinnamon liqueur with tiny flecks of gold).

This last item sends the diners into ecstasy, which kind of baffles me – especially since we don't even have any fancy orange soda and have to resort to making it with orange Perrier. I'm thinking, *Woo-hoo, it's just granita*. It's really nothing special. I'm thinking, If you're serving dessert, shouldn't you offer something that lives up to the rest of the menu? Again, I'm just the cook, so what do I know? But I'm seeing things that just seem curious to me.

I'm also learning a tremendous amount during the lead-up to these events. I learn how to meticulously segment the lemons and limes into perfect portions ("supremes"). I learn how to plate dishes properly – for instance, always placing the protein last, on top of the rest of the ingredients (vegetables or potatoes down first). I even learn how to stand properly when slicing or chopping: at a forty-five degree angle to the food, so your slices have a longer, more natural motion. I guess all this learning is also leading me to notice little things that I would change.

Take the sausage plates. I notice there's no sauerkraut on the plates. When I ask Dan about it, he explains that sauerkraut is an ala carte item and is ordered as a side-course. This seems kind of strange to me, despite the fact that the entrees are fairly inexpensive here, mostly in the range of eight to ten bucks. I would definitely do this differently. But what do I know?

I'm just the cook.

I also notice we're serving a beer-battered perch, which doesn't sound very German to me. And I also keep wondering why we don't have any chocolate on the menu? Isn't chocolate quintessential German dessert fare?

The grand tastings are also BYOB affairs, and to be brutally honest, the guests seem like a bunch of lazy assholes to me for not bussing their own dishes. And needless to say, for the tasting, I'm also the busboy.

On the whole, though, Chef Dan's menu is a winner. The schnitzel rivals the best schnitzel in Chicago, and this is a point of pride for me personally. In fact, my ability to hammer out a succulent piece of meat, bread it, and perfectly cook it, will serve me well as my career develops. Plus, Dan and I are building a good rapport with each other. This, I learn, is another essential part of a successful restaurant kitchen. The line cook needs to be the chef's right hand – connected almost psychically – so that every dish is an extension of the chef's vision and culinary concepts.

After surviving the grand tastings, I feel emboldened enough to gently make a suggestion: Why not serve the great pork belly Reuben as an open-faced sandwich? When I suggest this to Dan, he says, "Make one, and I'll try it." So I prepare one, and Dan and his sister sample it. "That's awesome," Jody says, wolfing it down, probably thinking that her brother made it. Dan is equally impressed, but he feels the traditional closed sandwich is better for the gastropub concept: an item easier eaten by people who are drinking beer and only have one hand for the sandwich. It's a fantastic dish, either way.

All of which begs a central question – one that will torment us in a strange way that first week, as we delay the grand opening due to plumbing and electrical problems: Are we a bar or a restaurant?

Lincoln Park is a party destination for many Chicagoans, and the sight of a new beer hall is like catnip for a bunch of rowdy twenty-somethings. Hence the decision is made, on a blustery, hot Thursday, one week after my start date, to throw some black tablecloths over the shaky-looking beer coolers, brace ourselves, and officially open the Hofbrau for business. By this point I am in a zone – coming in each day, going over the prep list, building the *mise en place* for whatever may come our way that day – and I am ready to roll.

One of the big attractions at the Hofbrau is the glass boot: these huge two-liter steins shaped like big Weimar Republic jackboots. They definitely lend an air of festive decadence, which the locals just love. Each night the noise out in the dining room seems to be increasing, the energy level spiking with each round of boots. I'm starting to wonder if the food is going to be secondary at this place.

Regardless of this early identity crisis, though, the chef and I are getting along pretty well, getting into each other's rhythms. And even though it's fairly chaotic out in the front of the house, it's smooth-running in the kitchen. I'm doing what I'm told to do as quickly and efficiently as possible, and Dan and I are working side-by-side on projects, and I'm really having a great time. Dan starts bringing in his favorite music – always Chef's Choice in a restaurant kitchen – and it turns out that he's really into the blues. It's not really what I dig, but God knows it's better than rap.

Throughout these early days, my friends would come in and marvel at my transformation from middle-aged businessman to professional line cook. Often they would make their way back to the kitchen and peer in at me in the heat of battle: "Hey Wayne, how ya doing?" they would call out. "Finally got a real job, huh?" Or sometimes a pal would stick their head in the kitchen and say, "Jesus Christ, it's so hot in here!" I would just laugh and say, "Whattya mean? It's great – it's like being in South Beach!"

After work, on the way home, I would sometimes stop off at one of my favorite neighborhood joints, Kelly's Pub, which is not far from the Hofbrau, and the bartenders and bouncers there, who all know me very well, would tease me: "You're a working man now, huh, Wayne? Just like the rest of us!" But the fact is I'm enjoying practically every minute of this new adventure, and even Chef Dan appreciates the schmoozing. He thinks it's great that people are coming in to say 'hi' to me, and it's even greater that they're spending money at his new restaurant.

But there still seems to be a lot of things that are slightly amiss at the Hofbrau.

For instance, I'm starting to wonder about the level of knowledge among my co-workers.

One day, Fiddlesticks and I are the extent of the crew. Chef Dan, who has finally taken a day off, has entrusted us with the operation. He leaves us with this massive prep list, far more than we will likely need for the evening. This is another thing I'm having trouble wrapping my mind around. Why create so much surplus food each day? It seems really wasteful.

Nevertheless, Fiddlesticks and I get to work. For the potato pancakes we have to grate a ton of potatoes. When I first met Fiddlesticks – a culinary school graduate – I figured she had much more experience than she actually had, and now, the more I talk to her, the more I realize she only has about a year and a half in the restaurant kitchens under her belt. She's still an excellent cook, however, despite the inexperience.

So we're grating these potatoes and I say to her, "It'd be nice to have an Oxo Good-Grips grater."

She gives me a look. "I have no idea what you're talking about."

"They're these graters with the soft black handle?" I tell her. "The best on the market, really. They cost like eight bucks."

She still has no idea what I'm talking about. I finally have to ask her, "Haven't you ever been to Bed, Bath, and Beyond?"

She just shakes her head. "Are you kidding? I don't have any money."

This gets me thinking about something else. If you are a professional in this industry, it is doubtful that you have eaten at many Michelin 3-star restaurants, or have even dined at the best restaurants in your city, because you don't have any money.

This goes for many *sous chefs* and chefs as well. Restaurant work simply does not pay enough to sample the fare at other top restaurants, especially when you're a recent graduate of culinary school. The sad fact is, a line cook's sphere of experience is very limited to the food they have learned about and tasted at culinary school, and/or the restaurants they have worked at. Other than that, for the most part, they really haven't experienced great food. Some think they know about it, but they really don't, and many just are not interested.

A few minutes later I ask Allison, "What's your favorite restaurant?"

She gives me another look. "Like I said, I don't have any money. I don't eat out much."

I begin to realize, more often than not, the inmates are running the asylum. In fact, by the time we reach our first weekend open for business, with the neighborhood yuppies and college kids pouring in to blow off steam and suck down a few dozen boots of Weiss Beer, I'm getting a really bad feeling about our fearless general manager, Adam, and his somewhat loose approach to restaurant management.

First of all, the guy has a major monkey on his back. He's always buzzed; he's sleeping on the dining room tables; he's got that disheveled, frat-boy-gone-bad look to his wardrobe. Second of all, nothing is getting done. Stuff is not getting repaired. Deliveries are not getting paid for. At one point, for example, I'm the only guy there with enough cash to pay the sixty-dollar tab for a produce delivery. And I'm making a grand total of nine bucks an hour.

So, on the whole, the general management is shoddy to say the least. And it's actually kind of sad, because, in my brief time spent with Adam, he has been nothing but a nice person to me. Friendly, jovial – maybe a little too jovial – but a decent person.

And it all comes to a head that next weekend.

Word has spread about the new German gastro-pub by this point, and we are getting slammed on a nightly basis. On this particular Friday, business is absolutely insane. By mid-shift it's so loud out in the dining room – with rock music blasting and people whooping and hollering – that I can hardly hear orders being called. Eventually it sounds like there's a Head Bangers Ball going on out front – with pounding noises and screaming and yelps like a herd of hyenas. I can't believe what I'm hearing. So finally I go out to see what's what.

People are literally standing on the dining room tables. Dancing, drinking, shouting, drunkenly singing – everybody's wasted on their huge boots of beer.

I just shake my head, and go back into the kitchen. "Chef, you have got to check this out."

"I gotta what?" He can't hear a word I'm saying, it's so damn loud now – or maybe he doesn't *want* to know what I'm saying.

"People are standing on the fucking tables," I tell him. "And I don't understand why nobody's doing anything about it.

I mean… people getting totally wasted and standing on tables? Is this such a good idea?"

Dan just shakes his head, his dream of creating a fine dining experience going up in a cloud of beer suds and school fight songs.

Where's the goddamn general manager? I go back out into the dining room. I scan the free-for-all, and then I see him: Standing on one of the tables, doing inebriated dance-moves, instigating the whole thing like a spoiled frat boy entertaining the degenerate alumi.

Adam.

All I can do is go back to the kitchen, shaking my head. I find Dan, and I look at him and say, "We're cooking in Animal House here."

CHAPTER 4

The crazier it gets – and it seems to be getting crazier with each passing day – the more I focus on what I'm doing. Every night Chef Dan is giving me more responsibilities, and I'm getting better and faster. Hit that pan with that knob of butter, put servings of Spaetzle on those two plates, get those slices of rye going on the flat top, sear off that Bratwurst, hit those sauces with some chopped parsley, bread those schnitzels. Done, done, done, done, done, and done. I'm ignoring the chaos out in the "dining/party room," and I'm minding my own business, and having the time of life.

"Get 8 Portobello's, 1 bottle of red wine and 4 quarts of cream." Yes Chef! And so my first sauce begins. Dan instructs me to sauté shallots and garlic in oil and then add the thick sliced mushrooms. When they begin to color, I pour the entire bottle of red wine in the huge pot, and let it reduce by half. Then Dan tells me to add the cream, all of it. Pouring the cream, a quart in each hand, two at a time makes me sort of chuckle.

This is an unbelievable amount of cream, runs through my mind; I would never do this at home. But then it hits me that this is a fundamental difference between cooking at home and a restaurant. I reduce the cream by half, occasionally stirring. When it finally reduces, I taste it again. My first sauce as a professional line cook, done, and delicious.

I'm also making more and more suggestions, seeing more and more areas for improvement and increased efficiency. Hand-slicing bread each day, for example, is extremely tedious. Chef Dan wants each slice cut precisely, meticulously, *exactly* the same thickness, every time – which is not an easy proposition, especially when you're dealing with a simple serrated knife. I finally talk him into letting me bring my electric knife in from home. The knife turns out to be a revelation at the restaurant, like introducing fire to a primitive tribe. Dan even starts using it to slice the cheese and the Pork Belly Reuben, a procedure which we originally found very difficult and messy and awkward with the chef-knife. At one point I even hear Dan murmuring cheerfully to himself, wielding the electric knife on a slice of Havarti, "Oh, man, this is wonderful."

On another occasion I'm flabbergasted to see Chef Dan and Albert the dishwasher smashing almonds for the schnitzel with big heavy frying pans. BANG!-BANG!-BANG! Almonds are flying everywhere, and I ask the chef if he wants me to bring in my Cuisinart from home. Culinary types usually call this food processor, a common household appliance, a Robot Coupe (pronounced "robo-coop"), which is the original industrial version, and it has many applications, but Dan is not a believer. "No thanks," he says. "I had a professor once who told me never to use a food processor because it gives everything a metallic taste." I just shrug and leave it at that.

In fact, the more I learn about the professional restaurant kitchen, the more amazed I am at all the macho posturing and superstition. At one point Chef Dan even says to me, "You know, there are some French chefs who believe the only thing you need to cook is a chef's knife." I kind of smile at that. "Yeah," I say, "I'm sure there are chef's out there who would do everything with a nail file if they could." But the point is, the bottom line is the product.

The most important priority for us is the food. And I'm amazed to say, somehow, even in the midst of all the start-up problems and pandemonium out-front, we are turning out quality food. Dan is a wizard with German cuisine, and I am loving every minute of line-cooking for him. I love the shop talk, and I love the camaraderie that's developing – despite the haphazard management. And more than anything else, I love putting out top quality dishes.

Take the Mussels Braised in Beer. This dish is phenomenal, and I really enjoy putting it together. You start out with a large, very-hot sauté pan, and you hit it with some butter, and then you throw in your shallots and garlic. This stuff will burn in less than thirty seconds, so you have to be fast on your feet. You throw in the mussels right away to slow it down, and then you hit it with the lardons (diced bacon), and then you add the braising-liquid.

The beer braise consists of a dark, malty, sweet German beer called Optimator, as well as bay leaf, peppercorns, and honey. And the magic starts right away with the mussels, as they blossom and open up and absorb all the flavors. You finish it with more butter and parsley. That's right, you read that correctly – more butter. In the territory of flavor enhancement, butter is the coin of the realm. You cannot use too much butter. Ask any chef.

The mussels are served with a dark rye bread with walnuts and raisins.

During these early days, dishes like this are really keeping me engaged, excited, focused… in a word, *happy*.

In fact, this is the great paradox of those early weeks working the line at the Hofbrau. Amidst all this chaos, I am actually feeling happy again – for the first time in quite a while. Again, it's the Zen thing. I had been under so much stress before starting here – with the uncertainty of my buy-out at the cookie company getting delayed over and over again and the ongoing havoc there due to the delay's – that the Hofbrau kitchen is now becoming an unexpected stress-release for me. Even my wife Andy is noticing it. She claims she hasn't seen me this happy in years. Her friends would ask her how she's handling seeing less of me at night; and she would simply smile and say, "Maybe we see less of each other, but he's so happy when I see him!"

This strange and wonderful phenomenon is also having *physical* effects on me.

First, my back is feeling three-hundred percent better than it had at the surgeon's office before starting at the Hofbrau. Much less pain. Second, I'm noticing very quickly that I can stand on my feet for hours without a break. Taking breaks is practically anathema in a professional restaurant kitchen – unless you're having a coronary or have perhaps accidentally amputated a limb – but I'm not only dealing with it, I'm thriving. Third, I sleep so soundly now that I'm even getting up in the morning without being a zombie.

Then I notice I'm losing weight, without working out. Part of it is that I'm eating better – having these healthy lunches on a more regular schedule before work. And part of it is because I'm metabolizing the food faster in the wake of all this physical work. I suspect I'm also probably eating less due to all the tasting that goes on while I'm cooking. No more five-course dinners.

Tasting is a critical part of cooking at a professional level. You cook with all your senses, but taste is the final arbiter. And as my taste gets more and more finely attuned, my cooking skills are rapidly improving as well.

The bottom line, though – as I move into my second week on the job – is that I'm made for this work. There is no doubt in my mind: This is what I'm going to do from now on.

• • •

Which is not to say it's easy or drama-free at the Hofbrau. On the contrary, as I learn more and more about line cooking, the place around me practically implodes with growing pains and staff issues.

The general manager is a disaster – every day appearing sloshed, dressed like a disheveled pirate, totally unacceptable – and no one is telling him to shape up. Finally, the owner makes a guest appearance, gives him a little talk and the guy promises he'll sober up. So one day he arrives dressed like a normal person, wearing slacks and a polo shirt, but unfortunately he's five hours late. The guy just can't win.

They finally lower the boom on the poor son of bitch on one of my days off.

The next day I come in and discover that we have no general manager. I can't say I'm surprised… but now what? We're approaching the two-week mark, and no one is getting paid. Dan is supposed to take over the management, but I'm wondering if that's a good idea. Things are leaking, jobs aren't getting done, and we still don't have any beer taps. And Dan has his hands full just managing the kitchen.

Ultimately Dan's sister, the server Jody, becomes the defacto temporary general manager. We rarely see Tom the owner. I learn he's got another restaurant project down the street, and we're becoming kind of an orphan. Once in a while, Tom will come in and announce a party of forty or fifty people arriving in an hour. No warning. No advance notice. And it's all-you-can-drink for ten bucks. By 6:00 o'clock the place will be filled with drunken people with no interest in fine food. Other diners are coming in, changing their minds, and walking out. I just shake my head and do my best.

By this point, the buzz about the restaurant is wearing off a little bit. So we're getting slower during weekdays, and I'm seeing some things that are really disturbing.

The servers and dishwashers are sitting around, smoking, hanging out in the dining room in front of customers. People are coming into the restaurant just to drink, and people are throwing up by mid-evening. The dishwashers are mopping puke out of the nooks and crannies, and I can tell Dan is dying inside. He's coming to the realization that this place is not going to be anything remotely like a gastropub.

At last, Dan goes to bat for the staff during Friday's service. He demands that the dishwashers, at least, get their paychecks. He tells Tom that he wants the staff to get paid first, and then the chef second (which, again, is indicative of Dan's integrity as a person). But it's like pulling teeth. Tom promises he'll cut the checks immediately. The shift ends and still no checks. Dan asks me if I want to wait for mine, I tell him I'll just get it on my next shift. But of course, when I come in for my shift two days later, there's no check.

Finally, a couple of days later, I overhear Jody confronting the owner during one of his rare appearances. "This restaurant is your baby," she says to him. "And you're neglecting your child."

One night I come in and I overhear Dan talking to somebody on the phone, suggesting that they review the menu, and I start worrying that he's going to hire another cook. Dan tends to play his cards pretty close to his vest. On this occasion he doesn't reveal whether all this interviewing noise is because I'm going to get fired or it's merely to help pick up the slack in the schedule.

I go home that night feeling a little insecure, so I feel compelled to go back on Craig's List. I just want to see what else is out there – just in case – which leads to a very important subplot to this saga, a subplot that will eventually change the course of my life.

For years I'd been frequenting this little Italian place down the street from my home; and I had eventually become friendly with the owner. I love Italian food and have always thought this place was one of the best kept secrets in the city. And now I see his ad.

I get the owner on the phone and I introduce myself.

"Sure, I remember you," he says. "What can I do for you?"

I tell him I'm working in the industry now as a line cook, and I may or may not be available. "But I've always liked your place," I tell him. "And I just wanted to have a talk in case something comes up."

There's a pause. "That's great," he says, "but I'm not really looking for a chef right now."

"That's okay," I say. "I'm not really a chef, I'm just a line cook. But I really like your food, and I'd love to sit down and talk some time."

"Yeah, sure," he says. "Any time you want to come in, that'd be great. I'm only paying like... well... I'm sure it's less than you're making."

"I'm only making nine dollars an hour, so pay's not the issue, believe me."

He laughs and tells me he'd love to sit down and talk any time.

I thank him and tell him I'll be in touch. Now I'm thinking: Wow, in less than a month I've made only two phone calls and in both cases the guy on the other end is interested in hiring me. Who knew getting a job as a cook was so damn easy?

The next night, I go into the Hofbrau for my shift. I have to know what's going on. Like I said, I'm a businessman at heart and I don't like uncertainty – not if there's anything I can do about it. So I decide once again to be as direct and honest with Chef Dan as possible. At the end of the night, I wait for the right moment and I take him aside. "Okay, so, now that I've been here for a couple of weeks," I say, cutting to the chase, "I was just wondering what your plans are? For me? For the future?"

Again, almost without hesitation, almost as though he had been thinking about this all along, he says, "Wayne, what I want you to do is write down every recipe you don't already know."

I stare at him for a moment, taken by surprise, and he goes on to explain that he wants to teach me whatever I haven't yet learned on the menu and the prep list. "I want to do this," he says, "because in about two weeks I'm going away for a few days and you're going to be in charge."

I'm nodding and grinning now, amused by the fact that I had gotten so jacked up about the whole thing.

"I'm hiring another cook named Melissa, who I know from culinary school, to help you," he adds, "because even *I* can't handle this place alone, and Fiddlesticks can only come in a couple of times while I'm gone."

I tell him I appreciate the confidence and I'll work really hard to prepare for it.

He looks at me without a trace of irony on his face. "I'm doing this, Wayne, because I really feel you're mature enough to handle it."

That night I brag to my wife that my boss feels I'm *mature* enough to be in charge, and the woman practically passes out from laughing.

The following Monday, Dan takes the night off, and I get my first taste of taking the wheel in the kitchen. I end up cooking alongside Fiddlesticks. By this point, I know the menu pretty well, as well as the prep list. In fact I'm becoming almost more of a *sous chef* than a cook, since I'm starting to do a lot of the Chef's work. It's not that busy, and we handle it fine. We manage to churn out something like fifty plates before it's all said and done. Sausage plates, scores of Schnitzel, Rouladens, Braised Duck with red cabbge bread pudding, Reubens, Mussels, and a bunch of Spaetzle dishes. And despite all the bedlam up front, I'm continuing to learn skills, cooking techniques, and tricks of the trade.

Fiddlesticks teaches me how to better "sauce" dishes, and how to know when a pan sauce is done. She shows me how to keep sauces from breaking – which is the point at which the sauce begins to separate into greasy pools – and she also shows me how to fix a broken sauce by adding in more liquid.

Born into a well-to-do family, whose patriarch wanted her to get a degree in *something*, Fiddlesticks had always wanted to cook. So she opted for a four-year culinary degree from Kendall College, which she found fairly worthless. After school she managed to get work as a professional cook, albeit on the minimum wage entry-level treadmill. She is a hard worker, though – a serious cook – and I really appreciate working alongside her. Strangely, I never find out for sure if she is Dan's girlfriend or not. This is par for the course in a restaurant.

Rumors and hearsay rule the day.

Supervising the kitchen that night, I really get a sense of sitting behind the wheel of the family car for the fist time, and taking it for a spin, and noticing a lot of squeaks and rattles.

As time goes on we're freezing and thawing and refreezing unused product, and I'm wondering how far you can push that food envelope. I'm seeing a lot of food being thrown away – for reasons that never quite make sense to me – and I'm learning about serving sub-par items such as our potato pancakes, which are sitting for hours and turning the color of mildew. We keep poached eggs ready for the Lyonnaise-style salad, but unfortunately nobody is ordering the salads, so the eggs are just sitting there and turning into Play-Dough. The thinly sliced cucumbers are turning to water. The Rouladen has gone from red to dark brown without being cooked. Certain entrees are not moving. I'm kind of baffled by the strategy, or lack of it.

Plus, I'm spending an incredible amount of time prepping stuff that rarely gets used. Take the candied lemon peels. Here's a perfect example. You have to carefully slice the peels into strips, and then you have to bring them to a boil. You have to let them cool, and then bring the water back up to boiling – three times, for some reason – changing the water each time. Then you submerge them in a simple syrup, then let them cool, then roll them in sugar, and finally – *finally* – you have these delicate little garnishes. All for the Granita, which no one is ordering.

For some reason, Chef Dan keeps giving us these enormous prep lists, and I'm trying to not think about the waste. We're prepping way more than we need and throwing tons of stuff away. We're also regularly doing things "on-the-fly" now. This is a huge issue for a professional restaurant kitchen – and a bad habit to get into.

Normally, when a restaurant kitchen is purring along like a well-oiled machine, and a ticket comes in, the components for every dish on the ticket have been prepped in advance. The process of cooking is simply a process of "assembly" and preparation of these components. But the real world can occasionally throw curve balls: Maybe the server has forgotten to enter a dish for a diner in a large group, and everybody else at that table is now being served; or perhaps communication has broken down between the kitchen and wait-staff, and something has been promised that is no longer available. Whatever the reason, the situation necessitates cooking "on the fly."

"On-the-fly" is a red alert for a restaurant kitchen. It could mean there's no ticket, and the order is verbal, and you need to do it right now. Or better yet, you need to do it "ten minutes ago." For some dishes, you have to do the prep "on the fly." For example: If there are caramelized apples in the foundation of the dish, you often have to go get an apple and start slicing. If there are cucumbers, same thing: You go grab a cucumber and start slicing, often due to the fact that cucumbers are highly perishable. If they are lying around, they turn to water. On-the-fly is not the best way to cook for service, and it seems to me, in most cases, you should be able to avoid having to do this.

And this is just one of the many things that are striking me as "curious" about the Hofbrau.

The haphazard way the dining room is being presented is bothering me as well. The lighting is all over the map, one night dialed up as full and bright as a supermarket aisle, another night dimmed down so low the place looks like an opium den. There's no continuity of music, either. Wait staff and dishwashers are bringing their I-Pods in, and blasting Snoop Dog and head-banger rock at all levels. Some nights there's just dead silence. Some nights we're closed early, others we're open late. It's completely unpredictable. There's no General

Manager. Nobody's getting paid, so the staff is furious at the owner.

Rules are being made up as we go along. The seeds of discontent are being sown everywhere you turn. I can see it in peoples' faces. I'm really getting a sense now that something is about to give. Of course, at that point, I have no idea just how hard it's going to snap.

CHAPTER 5

There is a calm before every storm. It's that slightly queasy stillness, when the light turns a sick shade of green, and the leaves turn inside out. You can smell it. Like the faintest whiff of ozone in the air. And then you feel the first drop plunk on your arm, and you just know you better get the hell inside. Sometimes you feel something akin to this in a restaurant kitchen before a busy night. Other times you feel it in the air all around you.

That third week at the Hofbrau is a lot like this: I'm doing my job, and I'm sensing this discord simmering among the rest of the staff, and I can feel a seismic shift coming, but I'm trying to mind my own business. But you can definitely tell something is about to give. I'm ignoring it, and trying to stay in that Zen space.

I'm also becoming so well-versed in the prep list now that I could create it myself if necessary. I'm learning the dynamics of the day-to-day operations – what to prepare when, what you can prep early, and what you can't because it'll go south. And I'm actually feeling pretty good about the way my skills and technique are progressing. I don't really care about the paychecks taking so long, or the fact that we don't have a General Manager yet, or the fact that the staff is about to stage a mass mutiny, because, fortunately, I'm not in this for the money.

I feel sorry for the rest of the crew but what the hell can I do?

I'm also getting faster and faster on the line. I'm actually beginning to expedite the food now as much as Dan is expediting it. Bigger kitchens usually have a person on staff responsible for this part of the operation – especially during busy times. Acting as a liaison between the kitchen and the wait staff, the Expeditor organizes orders by table and makes sure everything is garnished and plated properly and everything is coming in and going out in a timely fashion. The chef or *sous chef* often fills this role in a restaurant.

At the Hofbrau we're flying by the seat of our pants, trying to keep the quality up while the place threatens to go down in flames around us. Dan is giving me detailed notes on all the dishes with which I'm unfamiliar. People are finally getting paid – and I marvel at my measly little paycheck, my first as a professional line cook – but it's a hollow victory, because nobody trusts the illustrious owner Tom now, and he tells everybody he'll try to do better, but the assurance falls on deaf ears.

Then one day I come in to discover that Dan is unexpectedly going to be a no-show that night. He says he's got food poisoning. He claims it's something he ate – maybe some spinach pizza,

70

maybe one of the lemon poppy seed muffins we've been getting from a local bakery, trying to push as a fancy dessert.

Whatever the reason for Dan's absence, though, it's an opportunity for me to carry the ball once again. Unfortunately Murphy's Law is in effect that day. I can't get the flames to light on the stove or the fryers, and I have to call Dan to get instructions. The butane lighter doesn't work, and it takes forever just to get all the burners on. But eventually it gets done. (This problem with the gas service turns out to be a recurring issue, and I start to suspect the owner is not paying the bill.)

Then, to make matters worse, we get slammed that night. A huge group of my friends come in, and I have to spin out seventy to eighty plates before the evening is done, and I'm working all by my lonesome.

But what happens then is probably the first true milestone in my education as a cook. By 7:00 o'clock I am completely in a zone. I am not panicking. I am not whining to anybody about it. I am handling it – taking each ticket as it comes in – and I am surprising even *myself* with my focus on each dish, getting the food cooked properly, plated properly, and out to the customers. Maybe there's even an element of ritual here – my first true test in the heat of that stifling kitchen – and I'm ready. I'm getting tickets for multiple orders of pretzels, sausage plates, mussels, smoked pork chops, and various schnitzel offerings – all with different cooking times – and I'm processing it, multi-tasking.

Then comes a lull.

Then it picks up again.

The tickets come in waves like this all night. Just when I get something done, I turn around and see a new ticket coming in for two pretzels, an order of Beer Braised Mussels, a couple of Brat platters, one Rouladen, one Weiner Schnitzel, one Jager Schnitzel, and a brown butter Spaetzle. This, I'm finding, is a typical ticket tonight.

So I start with the pretzels, because people want pretzels first, so I get them in the oven, and then I get three new pans on the burners and squeeze some oil into the first one and start searing the Rouladen on all sides, because I know Rouladen takes the longest to cook, so I have to get that going. I'm using techniques and lessons taught to me by Dan, as well as my own cooking knowledge now. I get the schnitzels going in two pans in plenty of oil, and I turn the Rouladen. Next I count out the mussels and have those waiting, because pan number three is getting so hot you need to hit it right away or it'll scorch. I hit pan number three with butter, garlic, shallots, and bacon lardons – the smoke rising instantly – and then I put the mussels in the pan, which cools it down a little. I put in the beer braise and cover that with an inverted cool pan as a lid, and I put the mussels on the flat top. Then I put the Brats on the flat top. Then I move back to the Rouladen and turn it, and it's almost ready to go into the oven, but not quite. All the while I'm thinking ahead. What's next? What's next? Raisin bread! Shit! I have to get that going, so I butter four pieces of bread and drop those on the flattop.

Now I've got everything working, and the heat is like a kiln. I could fry eggs on the back of my neck, and I'm drenched in sweat, but I'm totally in that zone. I go back to the Rouladen, which is now nicely seared on all sides, and I get that in the oven, while taking the pretzels out of the oven. I brush them with melted butter, put some sea salt on them, and put them up on the slide. By this point the schnitzels are brown on one side in pan number two – which I can tell by checking the edges – so I flip them. The mussels are starting to open so I cut the heat on those and add a spoonful of butter and a pinch of chopped parsley. The sausages are seared nicely and I move them to the oven.

Next I take a hand full of fingerling potatoes and heat them in oil on the flattop. I flip the bread. I cut the heat on the schnitzels and get a new pan going with a huge serving spoon of butter for the Spaetzle. Flames leap up like a fireworks display, as I throw in two portions of Spaetzle with my bare hands, the fire singeing my knuckle-hair. I hit the Spaetzle and potatoes' with salt and pepper, and I start thinking about plating. I reach up and grab plates from the rack, and I lay them out on the speed table. I check the sausages – touching them in the middle to check for doneness – and they're done. I plate up the mussels with the date nut dark rye bread. I quickly heat-up the mushroom cream sauce, then finish and plate the schnitzels – which are a la carte – and put those up into the window. The servers are already starting to take the dishes out.

I turn back to the Spaetzle and do the pan-shake to evenly cook them. I pull the Rouladen from the oven and put it on a towel on my cutting board to let it rest. Meanwhile I hit the Rouladen pan with some more shallots and garlic, let that soften, and then hit it with some red wine. More flames lick the air, nearly scorching my eyebrows. I let the pan sauce reduce, throw in a knob of butter, and let it reduce some more.

Finally I turn around and grab my sausages, flash some kraut on the flat top, plate the sausages, the bread, and the kraut, as well as the sautéed onions and roasted garlic, on two plates – and that goes up into the window. I whirl around to the red wine sauce and I see it's now reduced properly – the big bubbles turning into little bubbles – so I cut the heat, and then I go over and cut the string on the Rouladen, quickly slicing it on the bias. I take the potatoes off the flattop, plate them, top them with the Rouladen, and go head and sauce the Rouladen. Two plates for Spaetzle swing around in one fluid motion, and then I grab the pan with a towel, and I guide the Spaetzle with my tongs evenly onto the plates. All remaining plates go up on the slide.

Another ticket out, another wave begins to subside, but the surf will be crashing back any minute now. I wipe my face and get back to work.

There's an expression in the restaurant business: "I'm in the weeds." This is a place you do not want to be. It's the proverbial melt-down, the threshold point at which the cook's brain gets so overwhelmed with multiple tasks that it just shuts down. I've seen it happen with people and it's not pretty. But for some reason – and I discover this that first "slam" night – I'm not the type to get overwhelmed. Maybe it's the football thing. I know I just need to cook the food, and there's no need to panic.

For me the weeds are not an option. Even when I'm line-cooking the entire line by myself, I just keep moving my legs and my hands, and focusing on the sequence. In the food world I know my place. I'm no prodigy or superstar, but I am relentless. And that's how I get through that night alone in the Hofbrau kitchen: *By being relentless.*

You have to be.

Especially when you're about to face the changes that are imminent at the Hofbrau.

CHAPTER 6

"**I**f that son of a bitch doesn't pay me today, I'm leaving." Big Dan utters these words to me before our one and only staff meeting, and I am taken aback by the menacing tone, which is not exactly this guy's normal style. But that's the way it's been going. Tempers are flaring. Promises are being broken. Welcome to the jungle.

I'm not exactly sure when the owner finally pays his chef, but I do know that things are rapidly deteriorating beyond the tipping point at the Hofbrau, and Tom is trying to put a finger in the dike. He tells Dan he's interviewing potential general managers, and he's trying to do better. He finally gets the real beer taps installed. But we still only have two servers: Jody and Nina.

Tom finally hires a new General Manager.

A former waiter at Spago – who also claims to be a *sommelier* (wine steward) – this guy looks like a professional the moment he walks through the door. We'll call him "Sean" – a

well-dressed, handsome, fit-looking guy in his early thirties –
and let's just say, for most of us on the crew, he is a welcome
addition to the Animal House atmosphere: A GM who can
form complete sentences and who refrains from climbing up
on tables.

At this point I'm still keeping pretty much to myself, so I
meet the new guy and I don't say much.

Sean spends a few days getting the lay of the land. He's
definitely got his work cut out for him. Even the bathrooms
are a disaster – there's no partition in the men's room between
commode and urinal, and I can only imagine what the lady's
room is like – but Sean takes it all in stride and tries to hit the
ground running.

It occurs to me right around this point that my masters are
still trying to figure me out. The new GM, Sean, for instance,
cannot wrap his head around my lifestyle, and all the different
modes of transportation I use. Finally he comes up to me and
says, "Today you took a cab to work?"

"That's right," I say with a shrug.

"Yesterday you rode your bike."

I look at him. "Yeah, and I have a car, too."

The blank stare he gives me says it all. I'm a real curiosity
to these guys.

On another occasion, Sean comes into the kitchen and finds
me prepping for the night. "What are the five best sellers in the
restaurant?" he asks.

I look up. "Excuse me?"

"We want to put together an abbreviated menu with the beer list, and we need to include the top five dishes."

I give him my trademark shrug. "You probably should ask the chef."

He presses the issue a bit. "Come on, just give me your opinion."

"I don't know, um… Pork Belly Reuben…?" Another shrug. I'm not comfortable with this conversation.

He keeps pressing me.

Finally I look at him, and as politely as possible, I inform him, "I'm just the cook. You really should be talking to the chef about this."

He walks out, slightly annoyed, and I'm thinking this is getting a little weird. I *am* just the cook. My allegiance – as is the case with all good line cooks – is with the chef, the coach, the leader of the brigade. I don't want to be consulting behind Dan's back.

The next day, which is a Friday, I come in and there's a powwow going on between Sean and Chef Dan in the kitchen, and I feel emboldened enough to listen in. Sean is trying to convince Dan that the place should start catering to the Wisconsin Badgers alumni – all of them big fans of German beer halls and friends of Tom's – and we should do a "football" menu on weekends and really go into the sports bar fare: Fried cheese curds, burgers, French fries, the whole shot. *An interesting clash of cultures*, I'm thinking, sitting there, ever the silent observer.

Chef Dan just levels his gaze at Sean and utters a single word: "No."

There's the briefest pause. Finally Sean responds: "Come on, Dan, you already said you would."

"I'm not doing this," he says, his big chiseled face like a stone monument.

"Come on, Dan."

"I've told you a million times, I'm all about fine dining, and this is not fine dining."

It's getting pretty tense, so finally I chime in, very softly, very diplomatically: "If I might make a suggestion?"

Both heads turn toward me, and I can't figure out if they want to kiss me or punch me in the face.

"What if we make a football menu," I go on, "but we do it with things we already have on the menu — sausages, pretzels, sauerkraut, maybe Pork Belly Reubens?"

They stare at me. I feel like a kid at the dinner table who just told his domineering parents how to fix their marriage. Finally, Sean looks at me with a kind of irritated smirk and says, "I thought you were just the cook, and you preferred not to talk."

Another shrug. "Look, if I have something positive to add, then I'll talk."

The tension does not lessen.

Finally Chef Dan says with a sigh, "Alright, alright, I'll make the shit, but I won't like it."

He says he'll order the ingredients and products for the pub-grub they want later that day. And then it's back to prepping in our sweltering little submarine cabin we call a kitchen. All the while I'm listening to Dan mumbling: "We already got the tomatoes… you can use your electric knife to slice the fucking things."

But deep down I sense something has been breached with the big chef, something that might be irreparable.

Late that night, after finishing up, and getting together some of the stuff for the game day party, Dan and I are chatting, and the chef confides in me: "You know that owner, Tom?" he says, as though he's got a bad taste in his mouth. "He never calls me 'Chef.' If he's introducing me, he goes, 'And this is my *cook*.'"

That's all Dan says at that point. And I don't make much of it that night.

In retrospect, I should have realized it was a portent of things to come. A sign my life was about to change.

The next day is Saturday – my day off. I sleep in, and then have a leisurely breakfast with Andy. And if things are messy at work, the weather over that weekend is messier. Severe thunderstorms with large hail and heavy downpours are roaring across the upper Midwest. But the rain only seems to be turning Chicago into more of a Swedish sauna. By late morning, temperatures are climbing toward the ninety mark.

It is right around this point that I hear my cell phone chirp.

I grab the device, and I see that I have an incoming text from Chef Dan. Before I even punch the message up on the tiny screen, I have a sick feeling that it might be bad news.

Or maybe it's good news. Or maybe it doesn't effect me at all, maybe he's just texting me about something we forgot to add to the dreaded sports bar menu.

But the truth is, as I thumb the VIEW button, I know in some corner of my gut that he's not just checking in to text about the weather.

Sure enough, when the text finally glows on the little screen of my cellphone, I am not surprised in the least that it's the game-changer I've been expecting:

> Wayne –
>
> I regret to inform you that I am no longer associated with that bastard Tom Rothman. I'm not going to have anything else to do with his bastardized operation. But I want to thank you for putting in such a great effort – it's appreciated more than you know. Good luck, Wayne.
> – Dan

It takes a moment for me to absorb what I'm looking at. It takes a moment for it to sink in. Not necessarily because I'm shocked by Chef Dan's departure – I guess I had seen the writing on the wall weeks earlier. Hell, I don't blame the guy for reaching the end of his rope. He had a clear vision, and that vision got blurred by the constant stream of compromise, mediocrity, and lowered expectations.

On the contrary, the reason I sit there staring at the text is because of its implications.

The Hofbrau is now a restaurant without a chef. Its doors will still be open. Diners will still be coming for their upscale German food; students will still be coming for their boots of beer; and the Cheese-Heads will still be coming on Saturday afternoons to watch the Badger games and spend money on Burgers and deep-fried cheese curds. It is a ship without a captain, and there is truly only one logical candidate to take over for Dan as the chef, and do it quickly and effectively.

Only one person who knows every item on the menu, who can create a prep list that works efficiently, who has spent a month shadowing Dan's every move, making copious notes and learning the tricks of the trade. Only one person who is calm enough to keep his wits about him and keep the restaurant from imploding.

I look up at my wife Andy and tell her the news.

"What happens now?" she asks.

I look at her. "I think it's very possible they're going to ask me to take over as the chef."

"What are you gonna to say? Are you gonna do it?"

I give her my trademark shrug.

PART TWO

THE ACCIDENTAL CHEF

"If you can keep your head when all about you are losing theirs and blaming it on you, If you can trust yourself when all men doubt you but make allowance for their doubting too... Yours is the earth and everything in it, And – which is more – you'll be a man, my son!"

- Rudyard Kipling, *IF*

CHAPTER 7

Eventually I find out the story of what exactly happened on that fateful day I got the text. On that muggy, rainy Saturday morning, Dan arrived at the Hofbrau around 9:00 with his other cook, Melissa, all set to start prepping for service. Around 10:30, Dan said to Melissa, "I'm going to the bank; I'll be back in ten minutes."

By 11:00 the place was packed, with no sign of Dan. By 11:30, the restaurant was filled to the gills with screaming Badger fans ordering boots of beer, burgers, pretzels, and cheese curds.

And Dan never came back.

Maybe he wanted to make sure his paycheck had cleared, or maybe he had an epiphany. Or maybe it was revenge. Who knows? I also learn over the next few days that Fiddlesticks had bailed as well. It turns out that she gave her notice a couple of days before Dan did his vanishing act. Again I'm not surprised.

Whether or not she was in cahoots with Dan – or whether or not they were an item – I'll probably never know.

Meanwhile, I wait all day Saturday for a phone call from somebody.

Here's what is running through my mind: I've got my businessman's hat on, and I'm thinking about how I would re-do the menu. I'm thinking about a new business plan, and how I would present it to Tom and Sean. I'm thinking about something that is workable to keep the operation running – especially if I'm the only cook for a while. I'm crossing off items from the menu that aren't selling or that I don't think will work.

I'm crossing off the oxtail soup, the weisswurst, the leberkase, the German eggs – all losers. The almond-breaded chicken schnitzel, the mushroom schnitzel with the parmesan coating – both delicious dishes, but they have to go. Beer braised mussels, one of my favorites to cook, but nobody's buying, auf Wiedersehen! I'm cutting out the stuff that doesn't make sense and does not sell. I'm thinking about how I would change the pricing.

At that point, of course, I have no idea if I'm even going to be able to keep the cook's job – let alone become the chef. But I want to be prepared. So I'm making all these notes. Again, I'm not panicked. I'm not freaking out. This is the restaurant industry, and nothing surprises me. The fact is, I'm using the principles I learned at the University of Toronto, and later in the business world as an entrepreneur and executive. I'm preparing as though I'm going into a business meeting to make a proposal.

Which is exactly what happens.

The next day I'm at an outdoor barbecue at a friend's house. The weather has cleared, and it's a beautiful day. I'm telling all my friends about the whole mess, and people are laughing, getting a huge kick out of it. But I still haven't heard a peep from Tom or Sean. Nothing. And I'm totally vexed by the whole thing until I realize something: *I'll bet these guys don't even have my goddamn phone number.*

So I put in a text message to Tom Rothman: *Here's my phone number, Tom, in case you need to get a hold of me.*

Within ten seconds I get a text back from Tom: *Out of town, I'll have Sean call you.* Within minutes, my cell rings. It's Sean. "Are you still an employee?"

"What do you mean?"

"Everybody else quit."

"What?! Who cooked Saturday night?"

"The other cook, Melissa, and Pedro, the dishwasher. And then *Melissa* quit."

My head is spinning now. "Who's working today?"

"Pedro. He's making burgers. But they told us you quit, too. Are you still an employee or what?"

I tell him, "Absolutely I'm still an employee. I'm still totally committed to the concept and your success. I like working there. It's that simple."

The slightest pause. "Do you want to be the chef?"

I take a deep breath. "You know what, let me think about it. I'm working tomorrow anyway… so let me think about it overnight and I'll come in a little early and we can talk it over."

By the next afternoon I've got my menu all marked up, and I go in about 1:00 with the attitude that this is an opportunity – maybe my only opportunity to continue cooking professionally at a restaurant. At this point in my career – with only four weeks of experience – it's not clear to me that I could even *get* another cooking job. Plus, a new chef could mean a new crew. I truly need to play this situation out. And as I've learned again and again, good things happen when opportunity meets preparation.

So I sit down with Sean, and I start by stating that my approach would be to develop a menu that would both increase the dinner business as well as compliment the late night drinking business. He's impressed.

What he doesn't know is that I've only been in this industry for four weeks.

"Do you know any other cooks?" Sean asks.

"I know a few people, and I could make a few calls." I pause at that point. I had met a few cooks over the years that I really liked, and now I had two guys in mind to make my life easier. "But let me tell you something, these guys that I'm thinking of, they're good and I want to pay them twelve bucks an hour."

"Oh my God, no way. Twelve dollars an hour is way outta line."

"Look, they're making ten bucks now. I want them to know up front that this place is a little more upscale, a little more professional, than the place they've been working at."

Another pause. "What are *you* looking for in terms of a raise?"

"Hey, listen, I'm not really looking for a raise right now, I know money is tight, and I want you guys to be successful. Plus I know I'm saving you money by not asking for the kind of salary Dan was getting. But I want these guys to get twelve bucks an hour."

Sean isn't convinced. He suggests that we bring the cooks on at ten bucks and tell them we'll reassess in a couple of months. I'm thinking this is typical restaurant industry bullshit.

I give him a look. "Do you want this same situation to happen all over again in a few weeks? You have a major investment in this place, and you're nickel and diming your cooks? How do you sleep at night?"

He lets out a long sigh. "Okay fine. Fine. We'll give them twelve bucks."

So now it's real. It's happening. With a quick handshake I'm a full-blown professional chef.

Almost like an accident.

Problems, of course, start almost immediately. Albert the dishwasher is a no-show that day. I call him up, and he sounds kind of out-of-it, maybe buzzed, maybe just waking up from a nap. He tells me he thought I quit, and he figured there was no food service today. I tell him not only did I not quit, but I'm the chef now, and I'm looking to reorganize the crew. A lot of cooks start as dishwashers. Does he want to learn how to cook? He sounds semi-interested, and claims he knows a lot about food, so I tell him to come in the next day and we'll talk.

The wait staff, for the moment, remains intact. Jody, Dan's sister, as well as the hapless, incompetent Nina, do their best to slog through the next few nights. But I can tell there's rancor in the ranks, and I can also tell I'm going to have to deal with it very soon.

But the real challenge at this point is to build a new kitchen crew quickly, and also keep the place running during the transition, so I've got my hands full. I'm mostly concerned about line cooks at this point, getting dependable people in there, fearless cookies who will carry their weight in that hundred-degree steam bath.

Luckily I know one of the cooks from Kelly's Pub – a kid named Ryan – and I decide to call him up immediately and poach for him with the twelve dollars an hour as bait. He takes the bait and agrees to start doing shifts whenever I need him. Another young guy I know from around town – Scott – tells me he's also interested but says he'll check the place out first and maybe do a "*stage*" with me – just to be sure – which I respect. In the restaurant business a *stage*, from the French word for "probationary period" (pronounced "*stahj*"), is a way of learning new things by working on a temporary basis at a restaurant you've never worked at – and doing it for free. In other words, it's trading labor for knowledge and experience. In the United States the stage has also morphed into a sort of try-out.

Maybe I'm an unknown quantity as a chef, but twelve bucks an hour is a big deal when you're making ten bucks. You have to be a pretty good line cook to make twelve. So I'm feeling good at this point about my new cooks. I'm just hoping my luck holds out.

I decide to make one of the other dishwashers, Pedro, a cook as well. I understand he is starting culinary school soon, so it makes sense (to me, at least). Plus, the kid stepped up to the plate when Dan had bailed on us, and I give him a lot of credit for that. So it seems like the right time to promote him from dishwasher – something Dan had promised him when he started.

A word here about Latino employees: A huge portion of all restaurant staffs across the U.S. come from Mexico and Central America. A lot has been written and discussed regarding racism and mistreatment of the "Latins" in the restaurant business. I've encountered this now and again. For instance, one time a general manager tells me – when I suggest hiring a Latino cook – that it's a bad idea because then we have to "lock up the meat." He actually tells me Hispanic workers will steal his pork loins to feed his family. This is not only racist, but it's ludicrous to me. In all my working experience I have found the Latin's I've worked with to be honest and hardworking and very professional. They are the back-bone of the restaurant industry.

The next day, in fact, Pedro surprises the hell out of me. He comes in dressed to the nines in cooking whites. He's got the hat, the name embroidered on his cook's jacket, herringbone chef's pants, the whole shot. He really looks the part, and I'm thinking this is good, *he must know stuff*. But the moment I give him a simple task – julienning some onions, naturally – I discover that it's all kind of make-believe.

It's like a Halloween costume, because as soon as we start cooking it becomes apparent very quickly that he has absolutely no cooking skills. Maybe he's nervous. Who knows?

Here comes a ticket off the printer. I start searing a Rouladen in a pan, temping up some pork belly in some braise, and getting a Weiner Schnitzel started. A few minutes later I turn to him and say, "Pedro, gimme the peppermill."

He doesn't move. He's like a deer in the headlights.

"Pedro, gimme the peppermill!"

Still nothing.

"Pedro," I say, turning around and looking at him. "Can you hand me that long, brown thing right there on the that shelf, please?"

I'm thinking: *Oh well, maybe I can get him to the point where he can make a pretzel.*

A couple of days later, under fire in the middle of a shift, he takes off his apron and announces, "Chef, I'm not your bitch... okay?" This is a side of Pedro that is just hilarious to me. He's this little pipsqueak who thinks he's a gangsta. But then he goes on and says, "I think I'll just be a dishwasher again."

I stare at him. "Are you serious?"

He is.

Later, Sean and I talk to him about the realities of being a cook. Pedro comes to his senses, and he goes back to cooking. A few days later he does a complete one-eighty and tells me how much he enjoys cooking with me and how much he's learning. But I'm wondering about his prospects. This is a young man who wants to go to Culinary School?

Eventually I suggest to Pedro that maybe he should consider going back to his original interest: *computer graphics*.

The other dishwasher, Big Albert, is equally enigmatic to me. When I finally sit down with him and tell him I want to train him as a cook, I'm expecting him to be just as delighted as Pedro initially was, but again, in the restaurant business things are never as they appear.

"So what I'm thinking," I say to Albert, sitting across a bench from him. "Is having you cook maybe a couple of days a week."

He nods and looks at me through those thick Coke bottle glasses. "Sure. I've been a cook before."

"I have to tell you something, though. If you're gonna become a cook, there's no more sitting outside in the dining room, smoking during service."

"That's it, man, you just want to boss me around." His big, bulging eyes are flaring with anger behind his glasses. "You think you know everything!" he snarls. "I know how to cook. I'm a grown up man!"

"Calm down, Albert, for Chrissake. I'm offering to teach you some skills – a *profession*."

He gets up and storms away, and I just shake my head, thinking to myself: *Fine. Whatever. He can be a dishwasher the rest of his life.*

The fact is, I'm beginning to see a pattern with a lot of these staff people. It's like a pathology. I come to think of it as the "It's-All-About-Me" syndrome, and it rears its ugly head again and again throughout my tenure as chef. But I never quite figure out why.

The restaurant industry is America's second largest employer, outside of the government, with over thirteen million workers. And many of these workers are poor. In many states McDonalds is the second largest employer of people below the poverty line. These are good, hard-working people, supporting their families, and trying to give their kids a better life. I'm proud to be working alongside them.

But now that I'm running the kitchen, I'm encountering things from my co-workers, – attitudes, work practices, and lots of drama – that just make no sense to me.

And as the days go by, the encounters just keep getting weirder and weirder.

CHAPTER 8

One day, during this transition phase, I come in and discover that we have no gas service again.

I call Sean to give him the news. He asks if I have the "plumber's" phone number.

The plumber?

"No, Sean, I don't."

"Fine, I'll take care of it," he tells me.

Later, I'm in the kitchen, trying to do my prep, when this tall, lanky dude – who looks like a member of Spinal Tap, complete with the ratty ponytail and greasy jeans – comes in with a tool-kit, on his way to the basement, looking for the gas line.

He's there for a while, and when he finishes, he comes back through the kitchen, looks at me, and says, "Okay, Chef, the gas is back on."

I look at the guy. "Who are you?"

"I'm the plumber."

"The plumber? What are you doing here?"

He gives me a look. "I'm not here," he says cryptically. "And we never had this conversation."

I find out later that the irrepressible Tom has somehow figured out a way to by-pass the gas meter in order to avoid paying the gas bill. I'm guessing that somebody tipped the gas company off, and they've killed the feed.

But now the "plumber" has fixed that problem again – until next time.

All I can do is shake my head and go back to prepping for service.

Thank God, the one thing that keeps me happy, that keeps me engaged, that remains the one constant – as always – is the food.

The Zen of slicing, dicing, mixing, pounding, grilling, and sautéing.

During this transitional period I work really hard to create a fabulous new menu that works, that's manageable, that makes sense for our concept. One of the first things I do is add chocolate to the dessert list, a wonderful Chocolate Pot de Crème*, which is a luscious, rich chocolate custard. I create a "Black Forest"

---

* Chop 8 ounces of semi sweet chocolate and put it into a blender; add 1 cup of hot heavy cream. After a minute, turn the blender onto low, when the chocolate is blended, add 3 egg yolks and 1 egg. When it's blended add 2 tablespoons of butter and 1/2 teaspoon of vanilla flavoring and a pinch of kosher salt. Pour the mixture into small cups and put into the fridge until firm. Serve chilled or at room temperature

version, with the addition of macerated cherries soaked in Port wine and topped with whipped cream and chocolate shavings.

I also add a sausage platter; a hot ham and cheese sandwich; a Kalt platter of assorted salamis, ham, Landjager smoked sausage, pickles, cheese, and two types of mustard; and a soup of the day.

I introduce two new sauces: a new one that I call a "Reingau" sauce, which I named after a Riesling region in Germany as sort of a riff on the classic French white wine; a mustard cream sauce; and a delicious new cheese sauce for the pretzels, based on the British classic Welsh Rarebit.

My version of Welsh Rarebit*, which turns out to be a huge hit with people, begins with a simple roux of butter and flour cooked until it becomes a beautiful blonde color, and then you add Optimator, the German beer discussed earlier, and you reduce it by two-thirds. Then you blend in the Worcestershire sauce, spicy mustard, cheddar cheese, and add salt and pepper. And it just becomes this utterly decadent, thick, creamy marriage of flavors that turns the hot, giant pretzel into a religious experience. The sauce proves so popular, I start to add it to Spaetzle, creating a German mac and cheese dish, which instantly becomes a big hit.

---

* Butter and flour - 1 tablespoon each; 1 cup of Optimator Beer or dark ale; 2 Tablespoons Worcestershire sauce; 1 tablespoon of spicy mustard; 1 pound cheddar cheese or Merkt's sharp cheddar spread, salt and pepper to taste.

I'm also talking to and learning more and more from the purveyors we're using. Take the meats, for instance. Because we're walking that fine line of a Gastropub, and we've got these Badger fans lining up now every Saturday by 11:00 o'clock in the morning, starved and jacked up to watch football, I want the gastro pub-style food to be great. I want to serve an exceptional burger. But I'm appalled to find out we're getting our patties from Costco. Nothing against Costco, but I've been a hamburger aficionado all my life, and some of the best burgers in Chicago, I learn after much research, come from a meat supplier known as Ruprecht Meats.

So I make sure we start using Ruprecht hamburger exclusively, and I start churning them out on Saturdays by the dozens and dozens, and they are *fantastic*. Juicy, flavorful, and tender, a big beef blast of a burger. People can really tell the difference, and this goes to the heart of what I'm trying to do.

In other words, there's nothing wrong with pub grub... as long as it's the Mercedes Benz of pub grub.

I'm also getting to the point now where my homemade Spaetzle is getting raves from customers. Making Spaetzle* is a craft akin to making pasta, and early on, Dan had taught me how to make it in the style of his German mother: You make a dough with flour, club soda, eggs, and salt; and you make it in stages, with a wooden spoon – old-school style – and it's really a stiff dough.

---

* 1 pound all purpose flour, 1 tablespoon Kosher Salt, 3 eggs, and 1 cup Club Soda.

You start by mixing the flour and salt, then adding the club soda a little at a time until it comes together. Then you create the little dumplings by forcing the dough through a contraption that looks like a coffee cup sliding over a flat grater, and you drop them into boiling water to cook. Over the weeks I experiment with several different devices, including colanders and even hand-cutting the Spaetzle, because making such a big batch with the grater device over a huge pot of boiling water could be classified as a form of torture. But I eventually find the best way to make these delicate little dumplings is with the contraption I find at Bed, Bath and Beyond called a grill skillet, which is a pan with holes in it for grilling vegetables, and it works beautifully. And people just love the stuff.

It's not rocket science, but it is an ancient culinary craft that I really enjoy doing.

All through that crazy, frenetic September, in fact – which passes in a blur – I try to focus on the food and leave the stuff like staff problems and ordering and making repairs to Sean and Tom.

But it's not easy.

Jody and Nina are making me crazy, dropping to-go orders a half hour before the kitchen even opens. At one point I ask them if they think to-go food doesn't need to be cooked.

Or they bury us in multiple tickets dropped at the same time, which should come in one at a time to keep the rhythm going and the patrons from waiting. Since the Hofbrau takes no reservations, you can go from ten customers to sixty, in a matter of minutes.

This would be tough enough in a two-man kitchen under any circumstances, but when they're dropping three tables at a time on us, it's a nightmare. This problem will come into play much more intensely in the coming days. Jody, much to my relief, eventually gets fired for not showing up one too many times.

There's also constant hostility from Albert the Dishwasher. I become a lightning rod for his contempt, for reasons that I still, to this day, do not quite get.

And it all comes to a head one day in a surreal confrontation behind the restaurant.

On that day I'm prepping with Scott – and by this time Scott is working out really well; he's turning out to be a really good cook and we're developing a great chemistry together – but unfortunately all is not well with Albert the dishwasher. He shows up really late that day, and I'm not happy about it, but I don't say anything at first. I just basically ignore him. The problem is, Albert's a real talker. Very chatty. And on this day, he notices I'm ignoring him.

All of a sudden, Albert blurts out, loud enough to wake the dead: "Some motherfuckers around here had to work until 4:00 in the morning!"

Nobody answers, and then he repeats it even louder.

I look at him, and I say, "Hey, you know what?" I point at a soup pot still in the sink, which for some reason was not washed the night before. "You mind cleaning this? I really need this pot now please."

He glares at me through those thick glasses. "Hey, man, I don't take my orders from you, I take my orders from Sean."

"Let me tell you something," I say very calmly, very steadily. "As a matter of fact, you do take your orders from me, now clean this pot."

He throws his hands up. "That's it, man! I'm not listening to you!"

He storms out. And I find out later that he went outside to call the owner, who, of course, would not pick up his phone. So then Albert goes and finds Sean and chews the poor guy's ear off.

I just shrug and go wash the pot myself. I need to make the soup, and that's just what I do. I start making the soup, trying to stay focused on what I'm doing, when Albert stomps back into the kitchen.

He comes over to me and he announces in this intense, angry voice: "We're having a *sit-down!*"

I look at him. "Excuse me?"

"Sean says we're going to have a *sit-down!*"

I give him a shrug and say, "Okay, fine, but we'll be having our sit-down after I finish this soup."

Sean comes into the kitchen and suggests we adjourn to the alley.

This might sound a little sinister, but it's not. We're not going outside to have a brawl. The alley is like the cone of silence for the restaurant, the place we have private conversations.

We go outside. The night air is cool and crisp. The El train runs nearby, so every few seconds this tornado of steel-on-steel roars past us, punctuating the tension. I start to say something when Albert starts snarling at me: "You don't respect me, motherfucker!"

"Calm down, Albert."

"I'm a man, I got children!" he says, losing control. He looks at Sean. "He disrespects me, man! He got the job here because of me! I told Dan to hire him! I should be his motherfuckin' boss!"

I'm just standing there, bristling at all this, completely taken aback, and thinking: *Holy shit, this thing could get ugly real fast.*

Sean tries to break in: "Albert, listen —"

"No, man, no! I could do *his* job, man. I could be *his* boss! I could be the motherfuckin' chef! He don't like me, man!"

"Albert, listen," I say, trying to keep my voice low and calm, trying to diffuse the whole thing. "I do like you. I got no problem with you. Don't I always cook you dinner? Make you food? I asked you if you wanted to be a cook? I got no problem with you. I just wanted you to do the pot, man. You gotta do your job."

"I don't have to do anything I don't want to do!" he growls at me again. "I don't have to listen to you!"

Sean looks at Albert. "Actually, you *do* have to listen to him, Albert, he's the chef."

Albert just stares, breathing hard, like he's about to pop. There's a tense pause, and I have no idea what's about to happen. Is he going to take a swing at me?

I look at Sean, and Sean turns to Albert and says very calmly, "Okay, Albert, go home. Take the rest of night off, and we'll get this thing straightened out."

I watch the dishwasher march away into the night with his fists clenched, still yelling at no one in particular.

Moments later, still in the alley, I'm telling Sean, "Hey, look, I didn't sign up for this program. The last thing I want to do is get in a fight with this guy and face a lawsuit. I don't need the exposure. I mean, I don't know whether this guy is bi-polar or he's paranoid, but he's got something going on and it's not good."

Sean proceeds to tell me that Albert wanted to call the police. He claimed that I was going to beat him up with a soup pot.

I let out a big sigh. "Sean, if I had a pot in my hand, believe me, it wasn't a lethal weapon. It was because I was making soup."

Two days later Sean lets Albert go. I feel bad for the guy, but what can you do? Albert is his own worst enemy. And it marks a minor turning point, because now, with each passing day, my kitchen crew is getting better and better, getting into a pretty decent rhythm. I'm even able to take some nights off. We're adding items, and making adjustments. The Brats, for instance, are taking too long. So instead of searing them on the flattop, and then in a frying pan and finishing them in the oven, I decide to start poaching them in beer and searing them off, which is a lot quicker and actually tastes better. We're becoming a well-oiled machine.

By the time the next payday rolls around, Tom looks at the figure on my paycheck while he's handing it to me.

"This seems a little light," he says, probably amazed that he's paying his chef line-cook money.

It must feel like paying the pilot of the airliner minimum wage.

I remind him that I only make nine dollars an hour.

"That seems really low," he says. "Maybe we should be paying you more."

I tell him, "Look, I know money's tight for you right now, so why don't we wait until Christmas and then we can talk about a raise."

He agrees, and I can't tell if he thinks I'm nuts or he just hit the jackpot.

•　•　•

What I don't realize during those hectic early weeks of my tenure as chef is that we're building up to something. In some ways, it's a tsunami, and it's headed my way, and I'm not fully aware of its implications. For me, it will be another baptism of fire and oil and heat and steam.

The basis for it started many, many years ago, in Munich, Germany.

In 1810, Crown Prince Ludwig and Princess Theresa organized an elaborate horse race to commemorate their marriage on October 12th. The entire country joined in the celebration, and a tradition was established. Over the next two hundred years, this festival — which has evolved, in Germany, into a sixteen-day event, running from late September to early October — became an international symbol for both Bavarian culture and beer-swilling bacchanals. It's called Oktoberfest — a milestone event for most Germans, as well as fans of German restaurants. And at my little place, it would test the limits of our resources and skills, and sanity.

CHAPTER 9

I go in early that first day of Oktoberfest. We're doing the prep, and we've got a new manager – Dylan, another twenty-something and male model, believe it or not, to work in tandem with Sean – coming in for his first night tonight. We even have a German band scheduled on this night – two guys in lederhosen for a festive touch – and I've got friends coming in. We've placed ads in the paper, and Lincoln Park is buzzing. People start rolling in by 6:00, at which point I'm out in front, schmoozing with my pals. I decide to go back to the kitchen to check and make sure that Ryan is okay and that the ship is braced for the storm.

The moment I enter that narrow, stifling-hot chamber of stainless steel, the wave hits. And I never get out of there again until it's all over. The tickets start printing non-stop.

I flame up the remaining burners that aren't on – *whoomp, whoomp, whoomp* – and the sauté pans hit the fire. I position myself in front of the sauté station – which is the most time-sensitive area – and Ryan lurches over to the grill, and *whap, whap, whap, whap* – rye slices start going down. Kraut is hitting hot steel, sausages are sizzling, arm hairs are singeing already. I'm starting sauces, and watching our new point-of-sale system (POS), ticking off the orders, and it's just chugging now: *bing, bing, bing, bing.* We're getting this stream of orders for the cold platter, and we're slicing the product on the fly, fanning slices of German salamis, ham, cornichons, Havarti and Landjager smoked sausage across the huge silver platters, one after another, and the accordion music is starting up, filtering down the back hallway like a taunt, and now the waitresses are coming up to the pass, screaming they need six more Brats – three veal, three regular – and five more Pretzles, while I cook entrees, and they need this and they need that, and Ryan is dropping what he's doing, and he's starting new dishes as a result, and I'm yelling at him to stop listening to the servers. I want them to go through me so I can "expo" the orders properly, but he's freaking out now, and before you can say *Auf Wiedersehen*, we've got sauté pans going and every burner and every square inch of oven space, deep-fryer and grill is occupied, and the heat is roaring, it's a wild animal clawing at our faces, and the tickets are still ticking off the printer, and we're both soaked in sweat and adrenaline. I'm running out of space for the order tickets now, so I grab some blue tape and affix it, sticky side out, on the edge of the pass – Dan taught me how to do this – and I start clothes-lining the tickets across the long blue ribbon. I can tell the waitresses are getting overwhelmed as well, as are the managers, who now have been forced to start serving as well, it is so busy, and they're all coming back all frazzled and wide-eyed, constantly changing orders, and adding stuff, which is now sending Ryan into apoplexy, and I start thinking, *This is not the way I want things to go, this is getting out of hand.*

"Ryan stop!"

The sound of my voice is like a cold slap across his face. He freezes and looks at me. "What, man? What is it?"

Over the din of polka music and voices, I speak very firmly and clearly: "You need to listen to me, I'm the expo and I'm the chef. I want you to do things in the order I tell you. And stop talking to the fucking waitresses because they're throwing everything off."

"But, but, but – yeah, man, but – we got this whole line of tickets!"

"I see it, Ryan. We're gonna get through it. But we're going to get through it my way, in the right order, and we're *not* going to freak out about it."

So he calms down a little, but the orders keep coming, and coming, and coming – I mean, it is a *tidal* wave. I've never seen it like this before. I start throwing open reach-in doors, and grabbing more product, going through the *mise'* like a whirlwind, finishing this with a squirt of honey mustard, and that with a dollop of red wine mushroom sauce, and shoving plate after plate up onto the pass, and then starting another pair of schnitzel, towel in hand, flipping the schnitzels still in molten sauté pans, and the sound of drunken voices singing along with "Roll Out the Barrel" is echoing, and I'm really getting into it, because I realize this is really cooking, line cooking, and I'm much better at it now than I was the *last* time I was slammed – the night I did over seventy plates all by myself – and now I'm also realizing that this is result of our reviews and our buzz and our great word-of-mouth. We are developing a reputation for great food and this is what happens. But I also realize we're running out of stuff. We don't have enough product. Even the dishwashers are getting overwhelmed, falling behind, and I start yelling: "I need frying pans, I need plates, I need everything!" The dishwasher is scrambling to get stuff washed, and Dylan, the new manager, comes in and he says, "What can I do?!" And I holler at him, "Go get that box of Brats out of the freezer and run some cold water on them – we're running out of food!"

It never lets up. All evening. It is just wall-to-wall out front, and the kitchen is a fucking furnace, and we are moving every second.

But the *piece de resistance* comes at the end of the night. It's getting close to the point at which we normally close down the kitchen – 10:00, 10:30 – and I'm telling the servers we're running really low on schnitzels, and there's no way we can re-prep. We'll have to basically call it a night after we go through the last five. Another ticket hits, and I repeat the new number for every server. Three Weiner Schnitzels and one Pork Schnitzel left. And I'm literally starting to shut stuff off, and stretch my weary bones, and wipe the sweat from my face. I'm about tell

Ryan he did a good job, when one last ticket pings out of the POS behind us like a little wagging tongue.

The order is for the following:

One Kalt Platter.
Two Sausage Platters
Five Pork Belly Reubens.
Five Weiner Schnitzels.
Thirteen burgers:
Three with no cheese.
Five with cheddar.
Three with Havarti.
Two with American.

We stare at the thing like it's a bad joke. It's from Nina. *Of course*, the fabulous Nina. I call her back, and I ask her, "Is this right?"

"Yeah, it's right."

"I just told you how many Schnitzels we have, and it's not five Weiner Schnitzels"

She sighs and without thought says, "Just make what you have."

"How many at the table, like fifty people?"

"No," she says, "it's ten guys, it's a bachelor party."

I let out a sigh and with a shrug I start cooking. Ryan is aghast. All we can do is start laying out six burgers at a time, and it takes forever to get all this stuff done.

The last ticket of the night.

We're turning everything off, and I say, "Ryan, I have to go out and see these dudes from this bachelor party. I mean, I'm a big eater, but I gotta see *this*."

So I push my way out into the throngs – and it's still jammed with people – and I find the table of ten. And what do I see? They have barely eaten *half* the food. Most of it is untouched, just sitting there, and for some reason it just kills me. It's not just the waste. It's the effort that we put into this food.

I find Dylan. "What's going on with Nina? Those guys didn't need all that food."

And then it hits us – almost simultaneously – as we stare at each other, and then at the bachelor party. Nina ordered for them. They asked her to order for them, and she simply ran up the tab.

This will not do. I like Nina as a person. She's sweet and funny, but this really bothers me.

I would have to make some more changes very soon, and Nina the Scourge of All Restaurants would be one of them.

CHAPTER 10

O rders.

In the restaurant business the ordering system of dishes is the crucial link between customer and kitchen. It doesn't matter how fine the cuisine is, if the orders are screwed up, the experience is lousy. And the finer the restaurant, the more rigorous the protocol. Some chefs insist on a seven minute turnaround – maximum – for an order. And this is complicated by the fact that many restaurants have as many as four different food groups that can come out on a ticket: grill, sauté, pasta, and pantry.

After the Oktoberfest slam, I decide to go through all the tickets from that night, every dish, and see what time it had come in, and from whom. And just as I suspected: The servers were taking order after order – from tables of six, tables of eight – and then, when they had a handful, they were punching them in all at once.

This is all kinds of wrong. This means that the first table is waiting ten minutes or more for other tables to order before their original order starts working. It's a cardinal sin for wait-staff to do this – especially at the Hofbrau, where we only have two cooks and six burners. But I'm resolved *not* to go through another night like the Oktoberfest Friday *ever* again without being prepared.

As it turns out, we don't see another night quite like that for the rest of my tenure at the restaurant, but I learn a lot in the aftermath, and I make a lot of changes to the system, and I really start stretching my wings as a chef. I have this backlog of recipes that I have developed over the years, and I start integrating more and more of my ideas and concepts into the Hofbrau experience.

Later that month, for instance, Sean asks me if I could cater a party at the home of an important customer. I'm intrigued and challenged by the task, especially since I'm starting to draw inspiration from the great brasseries in Paris, which are these cafes featuring full menus of rustic bistro-style food: soups, sausages, potatoes, *charcuterie*, and roast meats. Which is exactly what we're doing at the Hofbrau.

So I whip up a terrific array of stuff for the off-site party: Sausages, sauerkraut, potato salad, and this great goulash that I had taught myself how to make over the years. My goulash is not exactly German, but it's an interesting variation with kraut and spices, slow-cooked for hours. It turns out the goulash goes over so well at the party, I eventually put it on the menu. It becomes another signature dish at the place.

Meanwhile, my crew is evolving – or maybe de-volving is a better word – as the restaurant continues to define itself on the local scene. Ryan starts calling in sick, taking days off to deal with so-called personal issues, and I'm starting to get annoyed.

Little do I know it's about to get a *lot* more annoying.

. . .

Toward the end of October, I go into work and Ryan's not there yet. Dylan and I have a quick meeting, but I know I have to get started right away because I prepared a huge prep list the night before for today's service. I look at my watch. It's getting late and Ryan still hasn't show up yet. I text him a few times, with no response, I call him and no answer and then I realize – with that sinking feeling in my gut – just exactly what's going on.

I realize Ryan's going to be a no-call/no-show.

This kind of behavior, unfortunately, is not an uncommon occurrence in the restaurant industry: another sign of the "All-About-Me" syndrome. But I don't have time to get too upset about it; I've got work to do. So I abruptly end my meeting with Dylan, and head into the kitchen.

I plug in the I-Pod. U-2 blasts through the kitchen. I check my prep list and get to work. And there's a lot to do: I have to get a ten-pound ham in the oven; I have to make a three-pound batch of Spaetzle; I have to get the Reingau sauce together and reducing; I have to prepare the Dauphinoise potatoes[*]; I have to make goulash; chocolate pots; and much, much more. I have to get the equipment turned on, get things out of coolers, get everything in order – all by my lonesome – before the kitchen opens at 5:30.

To make matters worse, the inimitable Nina, Bane of All That is Orderly and Professional, brings in a carry-out order before the stove is even on. I just stare in amazement, wondering again if she thinks carry-out means uncooked. I'm getting pretty miffed by this point, and then it hits me. Another little mini-epiphany.

At first, I'm looking at this from only two angles: It's a ton of work, and I'm all alone. But then I realize I'm looking at it all wrong. My job is to cook great food. And that's what I wanted. I have all the stuff I need right here in front of me, and all I have to do is just cook it. All of a sudden, I'm happy again. It gets kind of fun. Cheap Trick are thumping away in the kitchen, and I'm sweaty as hell, but I'm doing it, and I'm going to get it done. Because this is what I do. This is exactly where I want to be, cooking up a storm, with Cheap Trick kicking out a victory jam:

---

[*] Take 1 lb of peeled Russet potatoes sliced into 1/4 inch slices, and cover with 1 cup of cream in a pot. Add 1 smashed clove of garlic, a pinch of nutmeg and pepper, and 1/2 teaspoon of Kosher salt. Bring to a boil, and cook until potatoes start to soften (about 10 minutes). Then place the potatoes shingled (overlapping) into an oven proof baking dish or loaf pan. Remove the garlic. Pour the cream mixture over the potatoes and bake in a 375 degree oven for about 50 minutes, or until the top is bubbly and brown

"Hello there ladies and gentlemen.
Hello there ladies and gents.

Are ya ready to rock?
Are ya ready or not!?"

As the weeks pass, Sean and Dylan are really trying to help me develop a protocol. They're hiring new servers, working on the front of the house, and trying to keep things humming along. We have a grand opening, which includes print media and local TV stations. We're getting consistently busy. And I continue to introduce new dishes, such as Bacon and Potato Soup, Lyonnaise-style potatoes with applewood smoked bacon and onions, and a Frikadellen, which is a huge pork and beef (3 to 1) meatball with pretzel crumbs, toasted caraway seed, and Dusseldorf mustard, the size of a major league baseball, which I stuff with Havarti cheese in the center.

I'm getting to know my vendors better, and getting better product in. I'm picking up little tips and techniques. I'm learning how other restaurants keep things "temped," how they hold their ingredients. I'm also using these "Bain Maries" – hot water baths – to keep the kraut and onions and cheese sauce warm without drying them out. I'm getting things down to a science.

I'm starting to really enjoy myself again, really getting into the chef thing. Big time.

Even the guys in the polka band are impressed. One night, after tasting the Bacon and Potato soup, they tell me they've been eating in countless German restaurants over the years, and this is the best they've ever tasted. High praise from a couple of polka dudes.

More importantly, people are writing about the place on the internet, and saying nice things about the Hofbrau.

With the advent of search engines in the 1990's — and the proliferation of the web into one out of every four homes around the globe — restaurant reviews have become the *di rigueur* destination for discriminating diners. But it's not just diners who are reading the critiques. Most chefs I know track the internet with the obsessiveness of CIA analysts. They get alerts, they check the blogs nightly, and they are relentlessly focused on what people are Yelping, Twittering and Facebooking about their dishes and their restaurants.

Much to my surprise, I find myself doing the same thing. I'm checking out the blogs practically every night. And lo and behold, people are raving about my food. I am delighted by all this: These are my first reviews, and they really lend a sort of credence to what I'm doing. They also keep me sharp. The food I'm putting out has my name on it now.

All of which is why I'm becoming a stickler for quality control, and becoming very cautious about my fellow employees and their ideas.

• • •

Scott, my line cook, is a wonderful kid, and a hard worker, but his passion and ambition — to be brutally frank — far outweigh his palate. One day he's stretching his food-wings a little bit and making pumpkin soup for Dylan, which he requested on my day off, thinking it could be a special soup for Halloween. Scott's using canned-pumpkin, and then adding stuff to it.

To put it mildly, Scott's soup is not what I would call a culinary masterpiece.

The following Wednesday is Halloween. Dylan wants to do all sorts of kitschy stuff for the holiday, such as including black-and-orange colored food on the menu. To be honest, it sounds disgusting to me. But I'll chalk it up to Dylan's youth and exuberance, so I tell him: "I'll think about it and try and come up with something."

But this is not good enough for the young manager. He also asks Scott to help with more spooky food, and Scott ends up making the Spaetzle black with some food-coloring. Upon seeing this I immediately eighty-six it. But Dylan is relentless, like a puppy nipping at your heels, and insists we offer Scott's soup. And that night, Halloween night, somebody actually orders the pumpkin soup.

So I go out front a few minutes later to ask the customer if he enjoyed the soup.

The guy looks at me. "Well, it was okay, but I asked for some Tabasco sauce. It really could have used some Tabasco sauce."

At this point I figure I had better have a little chat with Dylan.

I go find him, and I ask him if he could step outside into the alley.

We go outside into the crisp autumn night. "I take this job as chef seriously," I begin, shouting over the noise of the el train. "And when I took the job I did it on the basis that I would have total control over the menu, and that's the way it is."

"You do have control. What's the problem?"

"The problem is, when you put out crappy food it goes under my watch." I look at him squarely in the eyes. "And when people are writing crappy reviews on the internet, it is about *my* food. They don't know that it's you and Scott. I thought I had control over the kitchen, and if that's going to change, please let me know, and we'll figure out how to proceed from there. Because I will not tolerate putting out bad food."

He just gives me a shrug. "Well, you kind of shut me off about the black food idea, so I thought I would just ask someone else to help out."

"We had one conversation, and we did not come to a conclusion. You didn't give me time to consider it or discuss it with you further. You just went behind my back."

The El train clamors by us, almost like a noisy exclamation mark on my anger. Dylan finally concedes that it was not the best way to handle the situation. We shake hands, and I go back inside, wondering if this is actually part of my evolution as a chef – I care a lot about this place – and I take a lot of pride in what I do.

What I don't know at this point is that this attitude is going to take me to a new level very soon.

CHAPTER 11

As the holidays approach I sense another paradigm about to shift in my life. The Hofbrau is becoming a schizophrenic establishment – the food is uniformly excellent, I'm proud to say, but the atmosphere, management, and service is as bumpy and potholed as a Chicago road. Some nights servers just don't show up, so the managers serve, and they always sell a lot more food. On other nights, there's just one solitary server in the entire restaurant. And this single server has to take orders, pour beers – often into gigantic boots, which take forever to fill –and also deliver food. We have a diverse cross-section of people coming in – dinner patrons, bar patrons, football people – and I feel like we need some kind of continuity, some kind of identity.

Dylan is supposed to be running the restaurant now, but he's often at Tom's other place. And when he *is* here, he's trying to make life a little more difficult for me. He wants to add stuff like grilled-chicken salads to the menu merely because he wants to eat grilled-chicken salads. He's ordering product that is almost inedible, from really incompetent suppliers. Like the cheddar cheese from this place we'll call Horrible Food Service or HFS for short. I have never seen or tasted cheese this awful. It won't even melt smoothly, instead clumping up into a horrible mess. I start getting involved in the ordering process – which is something I had told Sean I did not want to do when I became chef – and now I find myself going directly to the importers and manufacturers. But the bottom line is, we're having a difficult time creating a hierarchy within the establishment – people are calling whomever they want when they call in sick.

I'm quickly realizing that this is probably an extreme example of what being a chef truly entails – micromanaging every last detail that has anything whatsoever to do with food. Amidst all of this "Sturm und Drang," though, I'm still improving the menu, adding festive entries for the holidays, and the crew is still evolving.

In November we bring in an experienced cook to help on the line, a guy with lots of kitchen-time under his belt at high-end places around Chicago. His name is Alejandro, and he's a real professional, a great cook. Unfortunately, he's also working at Tom's other place and is only going to be with me for a few weeks.

Around this time, Scott comes to me with his tail between his legs and says he's got bad news. He's got an offer for a full time job at *Les Nomades*, a highly rated, upscale French restaurant in town, and he's going to take it. I toss my towel over my shoulder and give him a smile. "That's good news for *you*, Scotty, bad news for *me*."

But I wish him well, and life goes on. Unbeknown to me, though, it's the first change in a wave of changes that will directly affect my life.

• • •

I place ads in Craig's List for new line cooks to replace Scott. Pickin's are slim. We're competing with top of the line restaurants that offer more money and more prestige. I interview several guys, and I finally decide on one – ironically also named Ryan. Ryan-Version-Two is a big kid, a southerner, who seems to know his stuff. He's a graduate of the Cooking and Hospitality Institute of Chicago, and has two years of experience.

Now, as the days pass, with Ryan-Number-Two getting indoctrinated into our system, I've got a crew that really works well. With Alejandro, Pedro, and a couple of dishwashers that I really like – things are moving along really well now. I'm adding festive dishes to the menu for the holidays, such as Sauerbraten, a four day brined roast served with a ginger sweet and sour sauce, creamed spinach, a port wine reduction sauce for the Kaessler smoked pork chop, and a wonderful cheddar cheese bacon chowder.

Unfortunately, Ryan-Number-two is not what he originally appeared to be.

For instance, one night we're getting slammed – I mean just a wave of tickets coming in – and we're getting a lot of orders for the new Frikadellen meatballs. So I turn to Ryan-Number-Two, and I tell him to start making meatballs. He hustles away and gets his latex gloves on and gets to work on the ginormous meatballs.

Meanwhile Sean comes into the kitchen and he's barking orders for hamburgers, so Ryan stops what he's doing and starts on the burgers. Then he goes back to the meatballs, putting his gloves back on.

I get an order for two schnitzels. "Ryan, please do two schnitzels now."

He looks up from his meatballs. "Why?"

I'm rolling my eyes now. "Because I want you to make the two schnitzels now for the experience."

He looks like a guy trying to juggle kittens now, and he's probably thinking, *Why can't the chef do the schnitzels? Wayne's not doing much, and I've gotta go through this Chinese fire drill with the gloves again.* His face suddenly drains of color. "I don't know, man, I don't know!" he blurts out all of a sudden with the desperate look of a lab rat lost in a maze. "I'm freakin' out, man! I'm freakin' out!"

I shake my head with a sigh. "Ryan, what is your problem?"

"I don't know – I don't know – I don't know –!!"

"Ryan –"

"I don't know how you guys do things around here! I'm freakin', man, I'm totally freaking out! I gotta go outside for a smoke!"

At this point, ordinarily, I would probably tell a cook who's melting down to calm down and shut up and cook (and by the way, you *never* walk off the line). But the problem is, I have to appease this guy a little bit, because I want to take a vacation soon, and in order to take a vacation, I need somebody who knows what's going on, somebody who can fill in for me. So I let him cool down and get back to work.

But this is definitely a defining moment for me, because I'm starting to really get worn down by this nonsense, and I'm starting to think about other options. And this is not the end of Ryan-Number-Two's disappointing performance. He starts calling in sick a lot, and he's really starting to make up a lot of bad excuses.

Plus, right around this time, my own journey takes an interesting turn.

What happens is, I get a chance to cook for a VIP that will eventually change the course of my career.

My favorite Italian restaurant in Chicago – and the one I have frequented most often as a customer – is a place called Coco Pazzo. Richly appointed in dark hardwood, blue velvet, and an open kitchen, the place is world renowned for high-end Tuscan cuisine. The chef there, a wonderful guy named Tony Priolo, has been a true mentor to me in all things food. Once in a while, as a diner, I would sit with Tony and say, half jokingly, "When I retire, will you give me a job as a cook?" He wouldn't skip a beat. "Yeah, absolutely," he would say, "come in tomorrow morning and you get eight bucks an hour." In recent months he's been especially helpful, offering to answer any questions I might have about the craft of restaurant cooking, and basically being a *mensch*.

During one of my nights off, I decide to go have dinner there with my wife. During the meal, Tony comes out and says hello. A thin man with a soft-spoken manner, Tony looks more like a professor of Italian studies than a master chef. And I'm tickled to see him. I tell him about my adventures, and he says he wants to come by the Hofbrau and have dinner. He says he really likes German cuisine, things like smoked pork chops (known as Kaessler), Weiner Schnitzel, and Spaetzle. And I tell him it would be an honor to cook for him.

We set a date.

Over the next few days I really pull out the stops getting ready. I go out and get a special sauce-pan to make the port wine reduction for the chops, and I plan a fabulous meal for the maestro. Finally, the night rolls around, and he shows up with his girlfriend, and I give him the VIP treatment. At the end of their meal, I personally bring out the chocolate pot de crème for his girlfriend. And later I give him a tour of our tiny kitchen. They both have a really great time. They linger at the place for nearly three hours.

Toward the end of the evening I look at him and say, "You know, Tony, this is a 'beginning,' not an 'end.'"

"I know, Wayne," he says. "I can see your passion. I see what you've done with this restaurant. I could make a call, and in a half an hour you would have your choice of ten top restaurants in this town that you could work at."

I am thrilled. This is the kind of validation that can only come from a real professional.

After weeks and weeks of working with cooks, hiring cooks, meeting other chefs, creating menus, supervising a kitchen, dealing with all the shit and trials and tribulations, I had hoped that I was cooking at a level that is considered top of the line. But I really didn't know for sure until somebody like Tony – who would never blow smoke about such things – told me as much.

He also offers, on that night, to have me come over to Coco Pazzo and work a day-*stage* with him any time. Tony is also a former saucier, and I realize I could learn so much from him, not only about sauces, but also about preparing dishes and cooking at a higher level.

This is a major moment for me, maybe even a turning point in my journey.

• • •

Not long after this, on one of my days off, I go over to Coco Pazzo to take Chef Tony Priolo up on his offer to work alongside him and his team, during a shift. Tony is gracious, generous, and most importantly, a meticulous, brilliant chef. I marvel at the teamwork in their beautiful, spacious open-style kitchen, glowing hot from the radiant wood burning oven. It's also as orderly as an operating room during a surgical procedure.

The day starts – as they do at almost all fine dining establishments – with prep.

Tony brings me downstairs to work with their in house butcher. He shows me how to clean and trim the Calamari (Squid) he's working on, and then cut the rings and tentacles. I take over for the butcher breaking down about fifteen pounds of the raw seafood.

Next it's back up to the kitchen to work with Raul, the lead prep cook, preparing stocks and the soup of the day. A former line cook, Raul recognizes me, and gives me a look of either surprise or amusement, maybe both. He asks me to chop up the onion, carrots, and celery, the vegetables that make up a classic mirepoix. After grabbing one of the house knives, I begin to break down the vegetables rapidly, trying to show some skills, wanting to fit in.

After finishing the onions, he smiles once again, "Wow, this guy really is a cook."

Service is starting and Tony has me hang out with the pasta guy, and I am totally impressed by the level of professionalism in this kitchen, as well as the symphony of cooking going on there during a rush.

Every sauce is built in the pan from scratch. The 'mise' is three times the size of mine at the Hofbrau, and that's just for the Pasta station. All the burners are on high and covered with sauté pans, and all the pans are extremely hot – super-hot. You have all this heat, and every sauce is very complex and different, with all these different components, some with meat ragu based or tomato sauce. Others with seafood or vegetables, some of them combinations, some with white wine, or different house made stocks, or brandy, or different herbs, and the slivered garlic is hitting the hot metal like an Uzi – *zing, zing, zing, zing* – and it is something to see. I am utterly mesmerized: this is real line cooking.

It is really an eye-opener for me. I realize you really have to have talent to cook at this level. I also realize I'm occupying a very special space – I'm in a moment – that's almost surreal.

I'm looking out into the dining room of Coco Pazzo, from the perspective of the kitchen.

And I'm doing the cooking.

After service is over, Tony tells me that perhaps after the Holidays I could work an evening shift. Needless to say, this really keeps me going, even as the infrastructure and irritations of my *own* restaurant continue to wax and wane around me…

…and big changes loom on my horizon.

CHAPTER 12

After Christmas, I take my first vacation in ages: ten days of R&R with Andy in the Caribbean. I take advantage of the peace and quiet to take stock. I'm a full-fledged chef by this point, and I feel like I've learned an incredible amount in less than five months.

On the beach, with sand between my toes, I start to think about my future. Should I start looking for other opportunities? Should I stick with the Hofbrau like a battered wife sticking with a deadbeat husband?

When I come back to work, in February, refreshed and reenergized, I'm focused on keeping the ship on course. I figure I'll stay at the Hofbrau for a year – max – and then move on to a finer dining establishment. So, *barring some unforeseen incident*, I've got another five months or so to take this place to a higher level.

But it ain't easy.

By this point, Ryan-Number-Two gets a second job working for a catering company, which, he confides in me, pays better than the Hofbrau. So one day he calls in at around 3:00, right before his shift.

"Hey *Waaaaaayne?*" the voice on the other end of the line drawls in my ear. "This is Ryan, man."

"Hi Ryan."

"I'm sorry, I'm real sorry, but I can't come in, man."

"Whattya mean you can't come in?"

"Oh, man, I got a catering gig tonight, man. Gonna get fourteen bucks an hour – *cash* – and I don't get paid from Hofbrau until next week."

I let out a sigh. "Ryan, what does this have to do with anything? You've got a commitment to this restaurant, and you need to be here."

"No, man, I need the money."

"This is your justification for blowing us off tonight?"

"Hey, man, I'm real sorry but I really need the money."

"Whatever, Ryan." I hang up with a shrug. Again I'm dealing with this strange, prevalent, selfish mindset, as if this is a perfectly ethical way to behave: *Hey, I just found out I can make more money tonight working somewhere else… so, you know, fuck you.*

Later I go to Dylan and say, "We gotta bounce this guy."

"Yeah, the guy's a Bozo," Dylan concurs. "He did terrible while you were gone, and he's late all the time."

So I go find Sean, and I tell him we need to hire a new guy.

Sean looks at me. "Yeah, the cooks are quitting all the time."

His implication is that they don't like working with me, so I say, "Yeah, well, maybe I'm a shitty chef. But when their paychecks bounce, I'm guessing it doesn't exactly enamor them to the place."

Sean reluctantly agrees that we need to hire somebody else, and we need to do it soon.

Not long after this incident, while I'm enjoying a night off at my favorite watering hole, Duffy's, my cell phone goes off and it's a text message from the restaurant. Now, keep in mind, I'm in no mood to deal with another crisis at the Hofbrau at this moment. I'm sitting back, working on my second Jameson and a nice *Romeo-y-Julieta* cigar. And I had even made sure that Pedro was scheduled that night.

Here's what the text message from Dylan says, complete with screaming exclamation marks:

THERE ARE NO COOKS IN THE KITCHEN AT THE HOFBRAU!!!!
THERE ARE NO COOKS IN THE KITCHEN AT THE HOFBRAU!!!!

I look at my buddy, Big Mike, and I say with an exasperated sigh, "No fucking way am I going in and cooking right now, no fucking way."

I go outside and call Dylan, and he assures me he told Pedro to come in, but Pedro said something about calling me, which he didn't do, and so I tell Dylan I'll give the kid a call, which

I do, and get no answer. So I call Dylan back and he says he'll figure something out, maybe grab one of the dishwashers to help out.

I go back inside the bar. And I share a laugh with my Mike about the whole thing. And then, out of nowhere, a voice with a very thick, French accent chimes in next to us: "Beat your cooks."

At first, I think I'm hearing things.

"You should beeeeeat your cooks."

I look over at this guy sitting next to us. "I can tell you're in the industry," I say to him.

"I am," he says with a nod, staring straight ahead.

"Hi, my name's Wayne Cohen."

He introduces himself, and lo and behold, I recognize the name – this guy is actually well-known chef.

I stare at him. "I've eaten at your restaurant. You're a great chef."

He gives me a little bow, and then repeats his sage advice: "You must beat your cooks."

"Yeah, the cooks are bad," I say. "But what about the servers – they're an even bigger pain in the ass."

He looks at me through twinkling eyes and says, "Kill the servers... before they kill *you*."

Personally, I would not recommend homicide as a motivational tool, but I would recommend looking long and hard at whom you hire to work on your line. And at this point, I need somebody I *know* I can count on, so I decide to hire my old pal – the same one sitting next to me that night at Duffy's – who will, at least, be dependable: *Big Mike.*

A huge guy with a jovial personality, Big Mike has a background similar to my own: He's been in sales for a number of years, but he has a deep passion for food. He does a lot of cooking on his own, and he makes a lot of complicated stuff, and he had a few restaurant industry experiences a long time ago. I also catch wind that he's been looking for a job in the industry for a while now – so I call him and ask him to join me at the Hofbrau.

He is delighted to join the team, and he proves to be very dependable, which really helps give our "bench" some depth. Especially since I don't have Allejandro any more – he's gone back to his old job at Tom's other restaurant.

So now I'm feeling like the foundation – at least in terms of my kitchen – is really on solid ground.

Or so it seems.

March rolls in, cold and gray – a typical Chicago spring – and I'm getting more and more restless. I'm thinking about my options. It seems like a tipping point is coming…

…and sure enough, it comes on a busy Thursday toward the end of the month.

Sean and Dylan have a calendar on the wall in the kitchen, on which they write down their special events and parties. I come in on Wednesday and see a notation for the next day: Thirty-five people for a Wisconsin basketball game. This is not a big deal, but it would still be nice to know exactly what the food needs are.

It turns out that the Hofbrau's owner, Tom Rothman, is around that Wednesday, having meetings with Sean and Dylan, and yet nobody approaches me about this booking. Finally, the phone's ringing, and nobody's picking it up, so I pick the extension in the kitchen. It's a guy from the University of Wisconsin, representing the group that's coming in the next day. He says he might be bringing in a few more people than he first estimated, and he'll be expecting a buffet-style service.

"Like sausage platters?" I ask the guy, thinking, *Boy, it would be nice if my managers gave me a little advance notice about stuff like this.*

"I don't know," he says. "I guess that's fine. They told me a 'big buffet.'"

"Don't worry about a thing," I tell him. "You'll have a great spread."

Now I'm thinking, Screw it, I'm going to just cover myself here and make sure I have enough food for seventy people. I call the sausage market and order additional product for the next day. We can make pretzels, mixed sausage platters, and goulash. I can create an amazing buffet.

Still no word from the management team.

The next day, I stop by the market myself on the way to the restaurant and pick up the additional stuff. I make sure we have enough bread, and I just generally cover our collective asses. I get to work and get started on the prep. Big Mike shows up for his first shift. It's good to see my pal, and I get him started on some prep work, and everything seems to be running smoothly. Game time is still several hours off.

Around 6:00, Tom Rothman comes up to me. "I'm really sorry, Wayne."

"What are you sorry about, Tom?"

"We're going to have a lot more people tonight than we thought."

Another shrug. "Well... I'm sure we can handle it. We'll do the best we can."

I'm trying to train Mike now, and also get ready for the party, as well as the regular service that night, when Dylan shows up, around 6:15. He finally tells me the program for the night.

"Let's see," he says, completely nonchalant about the whole thing, "let's just do three platters: a sausage platter, a Kalt platter, and a fried platter... and bring the first one out around 7:00... and that's basically it." *Hmmmm.*

Around 6:30 the floodgate opens, and people start pouring into the place. I mean, this is a tidal wave of red-shirted fans to watch the game and gorge on German food. Around 7:00 I come out with the first platter.

Tom comes rushing up to me like his head is on fire. "We need food! We need food! We need food! We need food!"

"This is just the first cold platter," I inform him, trying not to roll my eyes. "This is what I was told to make."

"We've gotta give everybody food right now!" He has a look of desperation on his face, the look of the zookeeper locked inside the lion cage without a whip or a chair. "Can you maybe make like a bunch of pretzels and we'll serve them to everybody like immediately?"

"I can do whatever you want but I was just starting another pla —"

"No! No, no, no… please make some pretzels like right now, Wayne, please!"

I go back into the kitchen and tell Big Mike — who's been working for the organization a grand total of three hours at this point — to get ten pretzels going. I start laying down sausages. And while we're cooking, the dining room is becoming absolutely packed. You cannot *move* out there. The game is in full swing, the noise is penetrating the walls, and the demand for food is coming at us like a battering ram.

Sean comes into the kitchen: "We gotta have more food! We need more food!"

"We're making the platters, Sean," I inform him with a shrug.

"You guys gotta work faster!"

"We're doing our best, Sean."

"Tom's looking like a real asshole out there to all these people; we gotta get more food out to these guys! You gotta figure out how to do this faster!"

"Look, Sean, we could keep talking or I could get back to cooking."

He keeps chirping at me.

By this point, I've reached critical mass, and I look at Sean. "Do me favor," I say. "Come over here for a second, come over here."

I take him over to the events calendar. "What's that say?" I ask rhetorically, pointing at the Thursday party for thirty-five. "It says thirty-five people. How many do you think we got out there?"

He shakes his head. "We don't know."

"I've been told we sold over a hundred-and-twenty tickets. What I *do* know is, that it's not thirty-five. Now let me go back and finish cooking."

I go back to the grill and keep cooking. That's all I can do. Mike's doing a fabulous job, and we're moving the food out really quickly. We're knocking out enormous sausage platters, both hot and cold, and putting out the sides of sauerkraut and sautéed onions and plenty of dark and light rye bread.

We finally catch up, and by 9:30 or 10:00 the final buzzer sounds on both the game and the all-you-can-eat deal. And I'm kind of proud that Mike and I pulled off this kind of service for what turned out to be a grand total of one-hundred-and-fourty-five people.

But this whole incident just sums up to me what the Hofbrau is all about.

Great food.

Complete lack of thought in the managerial department.

• • •

After work on that ridiculous Thursday night, I get home and decide to contact Tony at Coco Pazzo. Maybe I'm fed-up, maybe I yearn for more experiences like the one I had in Tony's kitchen. Maybe I just want to connect with the maestro again to stay on the cutting edge.

Here's the message I send to Tony:

Hey Tony, How's it going? Here's my new number... What's your day off? Let's have lunch.

Regards, Wayne

Within A half a minute, my phone rings. It's Tony. We trade small talk for a moment, and I'm really flattered he called me right back, but I'm also curious, because he sounds like he's got something important to say.

"I have some really great news," he says.

"What?"

"I just resigned and I'm opening my own place."

My eyebrows go up, and I get a buzzing sensation in the pit of my stomach. "That's fantastic," I tell him. "You deserve it."

"You're the first call I'm making," he says.

I wait for it, breathless, my fists clenching just slightly.

"I want you to come over and work with me."

· · ·

Way back in July, that previous summer, when Chef Dan had nonchalantly offered me a job as line cook at the Hofbrau, I had called him back two days later to make sure I had heard him correctly. To make sure I wasn't imagining the whole thing. Now I'm having Déjà vu all over again. The same thing happens with Tony.

I call him the following Monday. "Let me just make sure I understand," I begin. "*You* want *me* to come work for *you* at *your* new restaurant."

"That's right, yes."

"Okay, great, I just wanted to make sure I heard you correctly."

"You heard me correctly, Wayne," he says. "I know you, I can trust you. You've told me how much you want to do it. You know food. I want you on the team; I want you on the sauces and the pastas."

"I'll do whatever you want, Chef," I tell him.

"That's fantastic, Wayne, because I think you're going to be great."

I'm kind of glad he can't see how big I'm smiling right now. Finally I sum up my feeling with two simple words: "I'm in!"

CHAPTER 13

Those two simple words – *I'm in* – begin a new chapter in my life...

...and I have plenty of time to prepare for it. Tony's new place, which is located in a busy, gentrified warehouse district west of Chicago, is still in the throes of construction, and won't be close to opening its doors for another couple of months. Plus, I can't just bail out on the Hofbrau. That's not how I operate – although bailing out on places seems to be standard operating procedure among most of the people I've encountered in this industry.

But deep down inside, I'm marveling at the way the universe has dropped this opportunity in my lap. I could not have designed a better scenario. Italian cuisine has always been a favorite of mine. Especially fine Tuscan or Northern Italian cuisine. And Tony's is among the finest in the city, if not the country. My plan has always been to step up to a higher level of cooking and cuisine after the Hofbrau, but do it on the line.

That's where I always wanted to be: Cooking on the line and being able to cook fantastic tasting food. I love the heat, the speed, the pressure, the physical challenge of it. And even though Tony keeps addressing me as "Chef" – I think we both know, deep down, I'm a line cook, through and through.

But before any of this can happen, I have to close out my tenure at the Hofbrau.

At this point, it's late March. I'm thinking I'll give my masters at the Hofbrau at least a month's notice. I'm also thinking it might be a good idea to connect with a few of my other chef friends, and maybe do a few "*stages*" at their restaurants before I start at Tony's place. It might be my last opportunity to get those kinds of experiences. The fact is, once I jump into line-cooking for Tony, that's it. That's where I want to stay.

But it would be good to experience some other top-of-the-line operations before I make that commitment.

At this point, I have no idea as to the kind of culinary roller coaster I'm about to undergo in the months before I start at Tony's place.

Meanwhile, back at the Hofbrau, I'm keeping my plans to myself. I'm still the chef, doing my shifts, trying to deal with meandering management. After a week, I just can't keep the news to myself anymore. On a Monday afternoon, I sit down with Dylan.

"I want to give you guys my notice," I say right off the bat, without much emotion.

"Okay." Notwithstanding his somewhat haphazard approach to restaurant management, Dylan is really a decent guy at heart who takes things as they come. The way he just looks at me and says *okay* really captures this guy's essence.

"You know what, let me tell you the situation," I go on, telling him about the chef from Coco Pazzo starting his own place and bringing me with him.

"Well, I know you love that place, Coco Pazzo, and I know you love doing this." Dylan is speaking softly now, his voice almost melancholy. "You've done so many things for us; I really doubt I'll be able to get a chef in here that works as hard as you."

"I appreciate it," I say. "And look, Tony's place is not going to be open for at least a couple of months. I'll be happy to stay, at least through April, possibly through May."

"Sure, Chef... that's great."

We shake hands, and that's that.

I spend the subsequent weeks at the Hofbrau training new cooks, stabilizing everything, and preparing to hand the baton over to a new chef. And despite the headaches – countless staff meetings, revolving-door staff changes, clueless servers, and a steady stream of special requests – I'm feeling pretty damn good about everything.

In presidential politics, there's a period of time toward the end of an outgoing president's term – after the November election, and before the January inauguration – during which the incumbent is referred to as a "lame duck." This affectionate term merely refers to the fact that the outgoing leader has very little left to do, very little juice left in his administration, very little power left to wield. Traditionally, presidents have spent this time coasting, pardoning Thanksgiving turkeys, working on their memoirs, and basically marking time. For some executives it can be a shock to the system, a proud old lion with no hunt left in him.

My last weeks at the Hofbrau are not even remotely like this: Not only do I feel like I'm making a difference – helping the restaurant evolve into the next administration – but I'm really enjoying myself. I'm getting regulars who adore the food, and are coming back again and again. I continue to get great reviews on the internet. And my new crew is becoming a well-oiled machine, and Dylan has found a top-notch guy named Ken to take over the kitchen.

My last day, I'm gathering up all my personal items and equipment that I've brought in over the months, saying goodbye to everybody, and generally feeling like it's high school graduation day, like somebody's going to ask me to sign their yearbook.

At one point, I stand back and take one last look at that narrow little kitchen where I cut my culinary teeth as a line cook. A lot of the stuff that's still there – you would see it hanging here and there if you went to the place today – I purchased and installed myself. There's the track lighting that I brought in after remarking to Dan that it feels like an underground cavern in there. Up in corners are the satellite speakers to which I hooked my I-Pod after Dan departed. From that point on, it was no longer Chicago blues, but instead, a mash-up of my favorite classic rock.

I cannot count the number of hours prepping I listened to AC/DC in there. I listened to Foo Fighters, I listened to U2, Clapton, Hendrix, and Cheap Trick. I have so many fond memories of kicking out the jams while we kicked out the Schnitzels and the Spaetzle.

But maybe the most poignant reminder of the my legacy as accidental chef at the Hofbrau is the menu that still hangs in the store front window in Lincoln Park – my own greatest hits. The Goulash, the Gratin Dauphinoise Potatoes, the Welsh Rarebit Cheese Sauce, and the Chocolate Pot de Crème – these are really delicious dishes, but they are also my body of work. I introduced these to Dan's already excellent menu...

...and that last night, as I make my exit into the rainy April darkness, reaching for a celebratory cigar, I turn and take one last look at the menu in the window.

Not bad for a linebacker from Skokie who started out dropping chicken in hot oil and flipping burgers at Mickey D's.

PART THREE

THE MAJORS

"Professional cooking is about repetition. Only by repeating recipes, knife skills, and techniques — and developing one's palate through repetition — can one get to the level of restaurant food."

- Chef Thomas Keller

CHAPTER 14

EN GARDE: ACT ONE

As we edge toward April, Tony's grand opening is still many weeks – maybe even months – off in the future. After dipping back into Craig's List for *staging* possibilities, I see a perfect opportunity at a high-end place right in my neighborhood we'll call *Mon Oncle Gaston.*

An upscale classic French bistro, truly one of the best in the country, *Mon Oncle* is renowned among foodies for the usual suspects such as oysters, various kinds of *pate',* Steak *Frites,* French Onion Soup, Trout *Grenobloise* and *Boullibaise.* It's interior has that rustic-lush Nineteenth Century train depot feel, with the dark walnut wainscoting, shaded sconce lights, country bouquets on pristine white tablecloths, and the *Plats Du Jour* blackboard on the wall.

I really love eating at this place. And I really want to see how they run their kitchen, and how they run their line. So I'm thinking: *What the hell?*

I go in on a Friday with my newly created resume and I sit down with the *Mon Oncle Gaston* chef, a middle-aged guy with an attitude we'll call Harry. He wants to know all about my experience at the Hofbrau, and I tell him the whole story, including the fact that I'm going to be working at Tony Priolo's new place in a couple of months.

"In the meantime," I tell him, "I'd like to get into a few kitchens – do some stages – and get some more experience. I've always really liked this restaurant. So that's why I'm here."

"Well, you know," he says. "We're really looking for full-time people. Summer's coming up, and our patio opens and increases our business."

"I understand, but you know how it is in this business: You always need good people. Somebody doesn't show up, you need a body, I'm right in the neighborhood."

A pause. He purses his lips, thinking it over, looking kind of *pained*.

There's something about this guy that puts my guard up, that I don't like, an uneasiness, but I don't make much of it at this point. I probably should have recognized the signs.

"This isn't really a teaching kitchen," he finally says. "This is a professional kitchen, and we need full time professionals."

I give him a shrug. "I understand, Chef. Listen. I have good skills."

His wheels are really turning now. He looks like he's going to pass a gallstone. I'm thinking, what is this guy's problem?

Does he have to take a crap? After a big sigh, he says, "Let me ask you this: What's your availability?"

"Well... I make the schedule at the Hofbrau, so I'm pretty available."

"Can you come in and *stage* Sunday?"

. . .

It happens that quickly.

I go in that Sunday, decked out in my chef pants and shirt, with my knife bag. Chef Harry's not there that day, so I work with his *sous chef*, Lynn, a stocky, serious, thirty-ish woman who looks like she could be a prison matron or maybe a girls softball coach. She gives me an apron and towels. "The station you're going to be working at is called *Garde Manger*," she says, pronouncing it in the proper French: *guard mahn-jay*. "It requires that you wear a dishwasher's shirt."

Garde Manger? I'm familiar with the term. Translated literally as "keeper of the food," the *garde manger* also known as the pantry station is not as romantic or important as it might sound. Traditionally the *garde manger* is in charge of starters, cold appetizers, shellfish platters, salads, and *charcuterie*: pates, sausages, terrines, etc. At Mon Oncle, the *garde* also does desserts, which adds a lot of work to the station. The fact is, though, I never really saw myself as *Garde Manger* material – salads are not exactly my passion – but I'm in for a penny now, I might as well be in for a pound.

The first thing I notice is how much bigger the kitchen is. But despite its size, it is unbelievably tight. Lots more fire than the Hofbrau. More cook tops, a gas grill, and more stations. But it has a real prison-feel to it, with no windows – every station very cramped and compartmentalized.

Big Lynne puts me through the paces, checking me out, assessing my knife skills, seeing if I work clean. She has me dice about fifty shallots and slice a case of mushrooms and make the House Vinaigrette from their Recipe Manual, and do all the standard stuff, and she sees I know what I'm doing.

Working clean is imperative to being a kick-ass line cook. Working clean means you're constantly wiping your surfaces, keeping your cutting boards spotless, keeping your knives and utensils immaculate. When you're really rocking and rolling in the kitchen, stuff accumulates very quickly, bits of herbs, chives, and shallots scattering everywhere, puddles of stock, things getting sticky, greens mingling, stains, rings, oil-slicks, spills, and on and on.

Keeping your station clean means you're organized, which ultimately means you're cooking better. Your *mise en place* stays orderly, you're more focused, the plates come off the line better, faster, more attractively, more appetizing.

Working clean is essential.

I guess I pass the test, because Lynne puts me on the *garde manger* station immediately. I work with a woman named Nicole, and she teaches me a couple of dishes – the butter lettuce salad with apples, Gruyere cheese, candied walnuts, and lemon vinaigrette; and the endive salad with roasted pear, blue cheese, walnuts, and balsamic mustard vinaigrette – and she has me make them that night whenever one comes up on a ticket. The place is busy that night, and I get a lot of practice making salads, and I also pick up a few more dishes on my own.

The *garde manger* station at *Mon Oncle* is like a microcosm of every other kitchen station I've ever encountered: Speed table in front of us, low-boys underneath it (with all the product), reach-in coolers behind us, and a big sink. One of the thankless jobs that the *garde manger* must do – one that I come to dread – is washing lettuce.

The process of washing lettuce starts with removing the product from the packaging, wadding up some plastic wrap, stuffing it in the drain, and filling the sink with cold water. Then you have to trudge downstairs to the cavernous pantry – a double flight, straight down – to get the butter lettuce, spring mix greens, the spinach, and the industrial-sized salad-spinner devices. The spinner is precariously stacked on shelves over the stairs, and I'm terrified, because I have to reach up, and grab these huge Lexan plastic containers and spinners, and I just know somebody – if not me – is going to take a header down these long, dark, narrow stairs. Then you schlep everything back up to the station. You sink the lettuce in cold water, let it sit, and then spin-cycle it in the giant spinner. Water is shooting everywhere, and you're getting soaked, and finally you store the clean lettuce in the low-boys for service, and you find yourself becoming the salad guy because no other poor son of a bitch wants to do it.

I breeze through my first shift at *Mon Oncle*, and I start to see how things work at a superb French bistro, a place with a very high-level of culinary craft, but with all the same kinds of foibles and fuck-ups you would find behind the curtain at any busy restaurant. One of the many things I notice right off the bat is a more pronounced hierarchy: The chef, Lovable Harry, is at the top… or is he? In this operation, there are corporate chefs on top of Harry, providing a ceaseless source of frustration. Officially the *sous chef* is below Harry, namely the person supervising me: Lynne. And everybody is telling me something different, including my co-workers.

The wait staff at *Mon Oncle* are mostly veterans, well-seasoned troopers, but many of them turn out to be total drama queens, who make a hell of a lot more money than the cooks. They also have a corps of smooth, veteran, Latino food runners, as well, who know their shit, and keep the flow moving and the rhythm clicking along like clockwork. The place is always busy, too, even on Sundays and week nights.

The *mise en place* for my station, most nights, is extensive compared to the Hofbrau; in fact, it's almost encyclopedic: squeeze bottles of house dressing, lemon dressing, blood orange dressing, citrus vinaigrette; pesto; lardons; two kinds of croutons; blue cheese; goat cheese; olive tapenade; chopped chives; chopped parsley; fine slivers of ginger; chopped tarragon; grape tomato halves; seafood cocktail sauce; Mignonette sauce; cornichons; pickled baby onions; shaved fennel; carrots; cucumber; celery; red beets; golden beets; red wine mustard; stone ground mustard; apple sections; Gruyere cheese sticks; fig jam; candied hazelnuts; red and white endive; mache; watercress; grapefruit and orange segments; grated and hard-boiled eggs; diced pear; grapes; French sea salt; and much, much, much more. And this is merely one station.

The ordering system at *Mon Oncle* is also much more complex and finely tuned than our seat-of-the-pants system at the Hofbrau. At *Mon Oncle*, like most high-end restaurants, it's a two-stage system: "order" and "fire." When a ticket comes in – there are printers at every station in the kitchen – the orders are placed, but they are not necessarily started ("fired"). It is up to the expediter – often the chef, but sometimes the runners – to "fire" an order. Firing an order means you cook it, now, this instant, and firing also sets the clock on the turn-around. Once an order is fired, you must have it to the point of "pick up" in a designated (maximum) amount of time. Sometimes it's ten minutes. Some time it's less. For all plates at my station at Mon Oncle Gaston, it is five minutes.

I fall into the routine at *Mon Oncle* pretty quickly, and soon I'm being told I'm doing great. At the end of the shift, Lynne comes up to me and says, "C'mon, let's go downstairs and we'll have a little chat."

We go down to their dungeon-like office, and Lynne sits down behind the desk, across from me, and says, "Look, it's obvious you know what you're doing."

"Oh… thanks."

"But you're only passing through for a short time?"

I tell her about my impending gig with Tony.

"Well, you know… we're short-handed at the moment," she says, kind of locking her eyes on mine. I can sense something is coming. "We'd like to offer you a job. For as long as you want to be here."

This scene is not unusual in the restaurant business. Somebody comes in to do a *stage* – maybe a cook looking for a new kitchen experience, or a recently-graduated culinary student looking for a job – and if that person is a loser, they get a limp handshake at the end of a shift and told "We'll be in touch" (*and don't let the door hit your ass on the way out*). But if that person knows what they're doing – if they show promise, or have a killer instinct – they are usually brought down the creaking staircase to the "office" for a little chat.

And they are offered a job.

I am delighted by this development, and decide right there on the spot to take the job… unaware that it's probably a big mistake.

The truth is, I'm not as interested in working the pantry at *Mon Oncle* as I am working the hot line. I want to cook. I want to see how the sauces go down here. I want to get a taste of that cutting-edge French line-cooking. But, as it turns out, I get marooned on Planet Lettuce. Nothing against oysters, shrimp cocktail, smoked salmon plates, *pates* and salads – I love eating them – but I just don't enjoy making them as a cook. But unfortunately, that is exactly what I end up doing, shift after shift: Lyonnais salads, *Salade Nicoise*, Belgium endive salads, house salads, leek and mache salad, butter lettuce salads, tomato salads, duck salads, steak salads, grilled salmon on top of spinach salads, and an array of desserts; *Crème Brulee, Tarte Tatin* with caramel sauce, chocolate pecan tart, chocolate lava cake, *profiteroles* with vanilla ice cream and chocolate sauce, chocolate mousse, and on and on. I am responsible for preparing over twenty different dishes.

Toward the end of that first week at *Mon Oncle*, I have had it with lettuce. The glove issue, for example, is driving me nuts. We have to wear latex gloves, and we have to change gloves every time we make a salad. So I'm spending more time wrestling with the gloves now than I am making food. By this point I'm also making everything on the station, including shucking oysters (which I've never done before) and making the desserts, such as the Bananas Foster Crepes, which is labor intensive but also quite delicious.

You take two huge scoops of vanilla ice cream and wrap them inside a very large crepe, while you're simultaneously heating the bananas foster sauce. You peel and slice a whole banana, mix that into the sauce, pour the sauce on top of the crepe and place the bananas on the side. Then you top it with powdered sugar and a "quenelle" of whipped cream.

There's not much space to do any of this, so quite often I'm improvising my techniques.

Take the Crème *Brulee*, for instance. For those unlucky few who have never encountered this delicious dessert, crème brulee – French for "burnt cream" – is essentially a rich custard topped with a layer of sugar, caramelized into a delicate, brittle golden-brown crunchiness by a broiler or butane torch. But the problem is, you need a certain amount of elbow-room to do it perfectly, quickly, and efficiently. This is not the case at Mon Oncle Gaston, thanks to the tight quarters, because you're torching the dish while you're holding it tilted in your hand.

Basically the space I have to prepare desserts here is very tight. There's a narrow space crowded with 2 lowboy coolers, two industrial microwaves on top, pots of banana's foster sauce, and an induction burner for the poached eggs for the Lyonnaise salad – leaving practically no counter space. And all this is situated in a high-traffic area, across from the coffee service, with food runners, servers, and busboys – and everybody else – coming and going along that path at an alarming pace during the dinner rush.

There's an industrial torch sitting in a plastic container attached to the counter which I use to caramelize the *brulee*, and I have to do it *in the air* – one hand holding the *brulee*, one hand holding the torch.

"HOT!" I call out as the wait staff scurries by – *FFFFFOOOOOOMP!* – the torch flaring, scaring the hell out of everybody. "HOT!" *FFFFFFFOOOOOOMP!* "HOT!" *FFFFFFFOOOOOOOOOOMP! WHOA! HEADS UP!"*

People are bumping into me, and I'm dealing with caramel sauce that's like molten lava dripping everywhere, leading to serious burns.

Despite the intense pace, however, I'm not really being challenged.

I'm also seeing some red flags: Sonja, a distinguished Mexican lady, who is the lead *garde manger*, is a good example. I first work with her on my third night at Mon Oncle, and even though she's a veteran and knows a lot, I instantly sense something is wrong. Although it appears that Sonja has a handle on everything, I find out very quickly that almost everything she tells me is different from how Lovable Chef Harry really wants things done. Also, I'm told by the *sous chef* that Sonja is "mean" to the other *garde manger* cooks. This I find hard to believe.

Finally, I'm in the walk-in with her at one point and she turns to me and says with this intense tone, "Wayne... Wayne... you have to talk to the chef."

"About what, Sonja?"

She looks at me with the desperate thousand-yard stare of a shell-shocked soldier. "Too much, too much!"

"Too much?"

"Too much work. So tired. You have to talk to the chef, we have too much work."

I just give her a shrug. "Sonja, I just started here, I'm not in any position to talk to the chef about anything. Come on."

"You must, Wayne, you must."

I tell her I'll see what I can do, but what I'm really thinking is, *This is so typical.* I get into this upscale place and I'm seeing the same kind of personality conflicts and drama that drove me

163

crazy as a chef at the Hofbrau. But there's a bigger problem here than simply dealing with a shell-shocked co-worker. The fact is, even if I wanted to go have a heart-to-heart talk with Lovable Harry, it would be about effective as going to see Godzilla to humbly request that he refrain from stepping on so many buildings.

CHAPTER 15

EN GARDE: ACT TWO

The image of the overbearing, arrogant, sadistic chef is almost an urban folk tale. From the wincing little midget in *Ratatouille*, to the psychotic perfectionist Gordon Ramsay of *Hell's Kitchen* fame, the screaming chef has become a staple of kitchen lore. But the truth is, every professional restaurant kitchen in the world, at the end of the day, reflects the personality of its chef. Some are warm, some are nasty, some are in between. At *Mon Oncle Gaston*, the personality is a seething stew pot of bi-polar, passive-aggressive paranoia and thinly repressed rage.

All thanks to the dulcet tones of Lovable Harry.

"Whattya doing?! – whattya doing?! – whattya doing?! – why are you doing it like that?!" he snarls when he sees me slicing something.

"You know what, Marc?!" he growls on another occasion at a young culinary grad named Marc, who has just has just recently

come on board. *"SHIT ROLLS DOWN HILL! AND YOU'RE ON THE BOTTOM!!"*

"C'MON! –C'MON! – C'MON!" Harry barks at me later when he sees me plating something. *"YOU GOTTA BE FASTER!"*

"YOU GOT TEN MINUTES TO FINISH THOSE TWO DOZEN OYSTERS!" he hollers at another point, during one of his patented count-downs for the shucking of oysters, which keeps everybody on edge, but certainly doesn't get things done any faster. *"SEVEN LEFT! SIX! FIVE –!"*

I look at him and almost crack a smile, despite the tension in the kitchen, because I'm thinking this: *What are you going to do, fire me, and then have nobody at the station?*

"HEY! – HEY! – WHY ARE YOU DOING THAT?!" he *shouts at me on another occasion.* *"WHY THE HELL ARE YOU DOING THAT?!"* I stiffen and I step back and I brace myself for the storm. And he grabs stuff out of my hand, and he shows me how to do it *his* way with the impatience and irritation of an abusive parent one step away from taking the belt to his child. I have never seen a chef with this kind of bedside manner. Which is not to say he's always wrong.

Most of the time Chef Harry's correct, and he knows his kitchen, and the information is usually good. The guy is great with a knife. He has terrific skills. He is a legitimate chef, but his vibe is absolutely ugly. And in my humble opinion, this kind of vibe is less efficient.

But what can you do? To paraphrase a recent statement by a hawkish politician, you go into battle with the commanders you have, not the ones you *wish* you had. Early in my second week at *Mon Oncle*, this is made abundantly clear when I get a call during a day off. "Wayne!-Wayne! C'mon in, c'mon in!" the voice on the other end growls.

"Chef?"

"C'mon in, Wayne! C'mon in!"

"What's up?"

"Sonja didn't show up!"

I just roll my eyes, and I go in, and I work the shift with a new young lady I haven't met yet – we'll call her Renee – who turns out to be a major piece of work. "I'm the best one on this station!" she announces to me early on. "You do what I say!"

Sure... whatever.

And it goes on like this for hours: *I'm Queen of the Station, so you listen to me, and only me.* The funny thing is, Renee is *not* the best person on this station. Not by a long shot. In fact, I find out very quickly, her bluster and bragging masks a lot of incompetence and inexperience.

During service one night many shifts later, after another pronouncement by her of her greatness, I finally ask her, "Have you ever worked in restaurants before?"

She's kind of hesitant, hemming and hawing, making something up.

I look at her. "Have you ever worked on a hot line? Have you ever really cooked?"

She starts launching into stories of her experiences at Culinary School.

I give her a nod, and I say, "Listen, you know what? You've never really cooked and I have. You know what; I have more experience than you. So stop telling me you're the best cook in the place."

She stares at me like her head's about to explode. Finally she just says, "I'm not talking to you anymore."

• • •

I'm thinking I'll put up with this nonsense for a little while longer, and then I'll be on the hot line. I have no idea, at this point, that they have no intention of putting me on the hot line. I keep coming in for my shifts to be greeted by new stagiers and arrogant culinary students telling me how much they know, and how much I can learn from them, and how lucky I am to be partnered with them at the *Garde manger* station. Plus I'm one of the lucky guys who gets to do both the inventory at my station as well as the kitchen floors at the end of a long shift. Which means I usually have to stay a half an hour later than the rest of the crew as I'm still making dessert orders while the other cooks are already into closing their stations. And Lovable Harry is big on floors. "C'mon, c'mon, Wayne, put your back into it!" Harry's coaching me now. "You're a big guy!"

Somebody shoot me... because this ain't exactly what I would call cooking.

One day, toward the end of my second week, I come in early, and I start prepping – slicing and dicing – when Sonja shows up. I ask her to start on the lettuce. She goes downstairs and starts fetching and washing lettuce.

Meanwhile, the day-time *sous chef*, Guillermo, is working nearby. A wiry little Latino with a long ponytail, Guillermo's a talented saucier and cook, a good worker and an all-around good guy, although most of the other cooks don't like Guillermo, especially the Latins. They think he is Chef Harry's boy, and therefore not to be trusted. However, I enjoy working alongside him in the kitchen, learning what I can from him.

So everything's moving along fairly well, and I'm prepping, and Sonja's washing lettuce. Every few minutes she goes back downstairs to the cooler, and comes back up with more products. I kind of lose track of her at one point – I'm so involved in my own work, having an enormous prep list to cook through – but I just figure she's down there getting more stuff from cooler.

And then I hear Guillermo's voice in my ear. "Wayne..." he murmurs, "...you are *solo*."

I look up at him. "What? No... Sonja's here."

He goes, "No, Wayne... she is gone. You are solo tonight."

"Gone?"

I just stare at him. How could this be? I find out later that Sonja just vanished. At some point along the well-worn path between the *Garde* station and the downstairs coolers, she simply took the off-ramp and fled the scene. Now I am on my own.

Why am I having Déjà vu all of a sudden? Where have I seen this kind of passive-aggressive behavior before? Fortunately,

I'm confident that I can indeed go it alone on this night, and so I just shrug and get to work. I have no choice. What else am I going to do?

It's a busy night, and we get waves of tickets, and I buckle down with laser intensity on my station. Total focus. And by the time the night is over, I bang out two-hundred and twenty-five covers all by myself, and I do it quickly and efficiently.

Up until this point, Harry and Lynne have been giving me static about my speed. Everything is about speed with these people. You would think that food quality would trump speed. But it's all about speed.

At the end of the solo night, I find Lynne and I say with a smirk, "How did you like my speed tonight?"

"Impressive, Wayne," she says with a grin. "Verrrrrrrrry impressive."

But I am quickly reaching my limit. For instance, Marc, the nineteen-year-old culinary school graduate I mentioned earlier – toward whom Harry has been lobbing constant verbal abuse – passes through my station for a short time, and is then moved up to the hot line. I'm beginning to see the writing on the kitchen wall. (Not that Marc is happy with the work environment; I find out later that the poor kid, after weeks of Lovable Harry's abuse, decides to quit by simply leaving a "fuck-you" note.)

To make matters more ludicrous, Lynne announces one day (when I complain about not getting moved up to the hot line) that I'm going to be made the *Lead Garde Manger*.

Great. Hardly three weeks into this job, and I'm going to be a "made man" at a station at which I don't even want to be working. Okay. Fine. I try to learn as many new techniques as I can. I learn how to shuck oysters without turning my hand into a pincushion. I learn how to uses different knives for different procedures, different tasks.

And I learn how to deal with a psychotic chef, whose station is unfortunately right across from mine in the kitchen, a man who's always on my case to move faster, faster, faster. Not that he – if his life depended upon it – could accomplish the same task at the same times repeated in his ranting countdowns. Ten minutes to clean that bag of shrimp, *or else, 8 minutes, blah, blah blah…*

Lead Garde, and the most experienced one on the station is proving its own kind of challenges. Not only am I pumping out the lion share of the orders because the new cooks have less Garde experience than me, and haven't mastered the huge menu yet. But the orders keep on coming and coming. I'm also now responsible for expediting the orders, and I can't communicate efficiently with some, because of language barriers. So I'm happy to see a new cook join me in appetizer land: A tall recent culinary school grad, proudly dressed in his *Le Cordon Bleu* school chefs jacket. His name is Brian. Chef Harry is almost gleeful at his arrival. Showing him around the Kitchen, and acting as royalty has arrived to our humble abode. At this point I've already started working on my daily prep list, and I'm not paying too much attention to the new arrival, but I do find this a very curious act. Surprisingly, Chef Harry stops at my station, introduces us, and tells me that Brian will be working the station that night with me.

I start to train him the way I was trained at this station. I teach him two salads and two desserts, which will be his responsibility during service. As we start getting busy, I notice that Brian is getting nervous. There is something about the restaurant kitchen that easily triggers, and sometimes short circuits, the nervous system. The combination of the relentless demands for speed and quality combine to ratchet up one's nerves, especially a rookie pretending to be a vet.

As the evening progresses, Brian informs me we have run out of poached eggs, a component for one of his two salads. He asks me what to do, and I reply "Poach a couple of eggs." Before I can give him any further guidance, he has disappeared from the station. I finish my orders and prepare to poach the eggs myself. Suddenly Brian reappears with two coffee cups and proceeds to crack one egg into each cup. Having put my dishes on the pass, I decide to watch what my Le Cordon Bleu trained co-cook is going to do. I've seen this move before on many cooking shows. He slides the eggs into the boiling water, and he then prepares the Frisee lettuce, crouton, and bacon salad, as I have taught him. Brian walks away again and reappears with a paper towel in his hand. This I haven't seen before. He walks over to the now poached eggs, lifts them out of the boiling water and places them on the towel in the palm of his hand. Intently watching what he will do next, I see him slide by me, then he abruptly stops, and stares at his newly composed salad.

Chef Harry is bellowing in the background, "Garde Mange where's the Salade Lyonaise, where the hell's the salad?!" Brian's hand is now shaking, as he has finally realized he does not know how to get the delicate poached egg on top of the salad intact. He takes a leap of faith, lowers and tilts his shaking hand, trying to roll the egg safely on top of this beautifully composed salad. But no, bad luck has struck in the kitchen yet again, the egg breaks, ruining the salad. Finally, he asks me what to do.

I'm already breaking an egg directly into the boiling water. "Make another salad, I'll do the egg."

"Where is that damn SALAD!" screeches Chef Harry.

"Two minutes, Chef," I reply. I'm thinking, two years of Culinary School, Forty Thousand plus dollars, and this kid can't get a poached egg on a salad. I remove the egg with a slotted spoon and safely place it on top of the new *Salade Lyonaise*, just like Sonja taught me.

Later, when service calms down, I tell Brian: If he has questions, he should *ask*. I want to help him. Before attempting techniques he may have learned in Culinary School, make sure they are going to work on the line. He seemed grateful.

Brian worked another shift on my day off, but called in sick for his next shift, leaving me solo once more. I never saw him again.

• • •

"Wayne! – Wayne!" Harry says to me before service one day, about four weeks into my stay at *Mon Oncle*. "C'mon, let's go have a talk!"

We go into one of his side dining rooms. "How do you think its going?" he asks, after sitting me down like he's the Godfather.

"I have to tell you," I begin in a confessional tone, "I think I'm going backwards now. I think I was doing a lot better my first couple of weeks."

"Why do you think that is?"

Another shrug. "I guess I just don't dig the station. I'm not really that crazy about the whole *Garde* thing."

"Well, you know, Wayne," he says, getting that phony paternal tone to his voice. "If you want to be a chef, *Garde Manger* is really important."

"I don't want to be a chef. I want to be a line cook on the hot line. I told you that when you hired me. In fact, I'm pretty sure if you told me I was going to be *Garde Manger* my whole time here, I don't think I would have taken the job."

"But Wayne, look, when you go to Tony's, you're going to have to work all the stations."

I give him a look. "I'm pretty sure when I go to Tony's I'm going to be on the hot line. As a matter of fact, I already know what I'm going to be doing."

He looks like a child about to pout. "Well, it's an important station."

"I know it's an important station, Chef."

"But —"

"If you want to know the truth, Chef, I just don't feel like making salads and cold appetizers is cooking. And there's something else." I pause here.

He looks like his face is going to crack apart. "Go ahead, tell me what's on your mind."

"I gotta tell ya, working with you is starting to stress me out. And it seems like it's stressing you out more than it's stressing me out. And I don't know why. Maybe it's that my station is directly across from yours."

He takes a deep breath. "Wayne, you gotta move. You gotta see the whole 'field,' and you've gotta understand the timing." He starts throwing out jargon at me, stuff that he must get from his corporate management seminars.

"Look," I interrupt. "I *do* understand. I'm used to a lot of prep, but before I came here I was also the person who prepared the prep list; here, I just have to do it. I bring a positive attitude to every shift. I give a hundred-and-ten percent effort. If my job is to make a salad, I want to make the best salad every time. I am a fan of this restaurant, and I think the food here now is better than ever." I pause here again, preparing to make an important point, and maybe even give him a little bit of my own management philosophy. "But you know what," I say, "the job of management is to get the most out of every employee, recognizing that each employee may be motivated differently. That's not happening here. I'm used to being the best employee, wherever I work."

He's quiet now, just listening, maybe even a little stunned. It's almost as though I've turned the tables on him, the teacher becoming the student. Finally he says with this fake smile, "You know what? Let's take this as a positive conversation, and let's stay positive for the rest of the time you're here."

This is the end of our little "chat" – and I realize this guy is clueless, and nothing is going to change, and he's going to remain an asshole long after I've gone on to greener pantries. So a few days later, I have come to the end of my tolerance for the pantry, for Harry, and for *Mon Oncle*.

I tell Harry I'd like to put in my notice.

He asks me to stay as long as I can.

Two weeks is proper notice in any business, and as much as I can stomach, so I give him two weeks. Ironically, on my last night, Lynn asks me to stay. I tell her, "Sure, I'll continue for a while, but there's one condition: I don't work shifts with Harry."

She just stares at me.

Obviously this doesn't fly.

Thankfully I have no place to go but up.

CHAPTER 16

SUPERSTARS

N
owadays, molecular-gastronomy is all the rage with adventurous foodies. Sometimes referred to as high-tech cuisine, this modern school of cooking utilizes the latest scientific innovations and molecular biology to transform traditional approaches to cooking. New dishes are created through avant-garde preparations, equipment, and plating. Some are whimsical, some are startling, and some are simply new and pleasantly surprising to the palate.

As June rolls around – and I learn that Tony has decided to hold off opening his doors until he gets his liquor license, which could take a while – I decide to make a reservation for my birthday at a new place opening up in Chicago that I'm extremely curious about.

Graham Elliot Bowles is a young super-star chef on the rise in national food circles. A big, beefy, tattooed hipster, this thirty year old prodigy has an impressive resume for such a young man, having kicked around Chicago for several years with some of the biggest names in the local restaurant scene. He was the Executive Chef at Avenues in the Peninsula Hotel, a four star restaurant. He's worked with Charlie Trotter for years, and also as the Chef de Cuisine at Tru, another four-star Chicago restaurant. A nominee for numerous James Beard awards, he's been featured in all the magazines and has appeared on the Food Network's "Iron Chef" and as a competitor on the wildly popular Bravo TV series "Top Chef Masters." He is a judge on Fox TV's "Master Chef" with Gordon Ramsay.

When I learn that Bowles is opening his own restaurant in Chicago, I have to check it out. The place will be called, fittingly, *Graham Elliot*, and is being billed as Chicago's first "bistronomic" restaurant. I guess what this means is simple American bistro fare elevated by scientific razzle-dazzle, as well as a sense of fun. Some people call it "food as art," but I never liked that phrase. I never wanted to eat a painting. But when I read about the menu at Graham Elliot's on line, I get really excited.

So one afternoon I go down to the near-north side to the gallery district, where the place is located, to see if I can get a reservation. I'm wearing shorts, a t-shirt and a baseball cap, and when I get there I recognize the man himself inside the window. The place is beautifully designed, with exposed beams, floor-to-ceiling windows, and hundred-year-old brick walls, but I can't tell if they're open or not... so I knock on the door. And Graham himself comes up and opens the door.

He's a big guy with cropped hair and very hip glasses. He reminds me of many of the offensive linemen I had battled against in my football days. But he is very friendly and unassuming. He tells me that they're opening up that night, and he would be happy to make a reservation for me. We chat as he's taking down my information. "You know, I'm actually a cook," I blurt out at one point in the conversation, thinking, *what the hell?*

"Yeah?" he says, punching my name into the reservation file. "That's cool."

I tell him about the Hofbrau, Mon Oncle, and my current status waiting to start at Tony's.

"Yeah, I've heard of Tony," he says. "The guy from Coco Pazzo, right?"

"Exactly... and you know what, in the meantime, if you need some help, I'd be happy to come in and *stage*."

He stops typing for a second and looks at me. "You mean like come in and just trail a guy and help us out?"

"Absolutely, yeah. I'm not doing anything right now. And I'd really enjoy it."

Without a pause he says, "Yeah, that'd be great. Sure. We could use the help. When do you want to come in?"

By now it's probably becoming apparent that one of the overriding themes of this book is this: If you have in-depth food knowledge, and some skills, and the passion, and the *cojones*, it's not that hard talking your way into professional restaurant kitchens. Even the best of the best. The work is there. You just have to be open to the possibilities.

Here's another example: It turns out a buddy of mine in my apartment building frequents the same health club as another top Chicago chef: Martial Noguier.

Paris born, movie-star handsome, and a graduate of the French Culinary Academy, Martial Noguier has, for nearly a decade now, been one of the most underrated chefs in Chicago. Bar none. The executive chef at a place called *one sixtyblue*, he has gotten rave after rave from food critics and guidebooks alike over the years. Ironically, the day after I meet Graham Elliot, my buddy calls me up and says one sixtyblue has lost some people lately, and he mentioned me to Martial. Martial wants me to call.

He wants me to call him?

Located on Chicago's west side, in the trendy market district, one sixtyblue is part owned by basketball legend Michael Jordon. Inside, it's plush, and sleek and low lighting – a place I have always admired – so when I hear my neighbor has the ear of the Star chef Martial Noguier, I'm thinking, hmmmmmmm...

I get on the phone, and I get the chef on the line. "Hi, Chef Martial, this is Wayne Cohen, a friend of John's"

"Can you work *Thursday?*" the deeply accented voice interrupts.

I practically flinch. This is just too easy. It should be more difficult than this. "Well, actually, I'm sorry to say I can't on Thursday."

"And why not?"

"Well, to be honest with you, I'm working at Graham Elliot's on Thursday."

"You're working with *Graham?*" He accents the word Graham with that wonderful, intense, musical, French lilt: *Grrrrrrrrrrrayham?*

"Yeah," I say, "I am."

"Then come in Friday."

"Well..."

"You must! You must come in Friday!"

So I agree.

How could I not agree with a great chef who speaks like this?

CHAPTER 17

AN EMBARRASSMENT OF RICHES

Over the next few days, as I check in for work at each of these top-line restaurants, I go from the sublime to the *sublimer*; and after working for Lovable Harry and his Band of Unhappy Campers, it is a refreshing change

The kitchen at Graham Elliot's is not super-huge, but it is brand new and beautifully designed: It's clean, it's spacious, a stunning red granite counter replaces the usual Steel slide, and there's a custom I-Pod system built into the walls to play a never ending stream of great music in the kitchen. The cooks are a different breed of kitchen crew than I'm used to. They're mostly in their thirties, each with at least a decade of experience. They're here because they want to work with a superstar chef.

I fit right into the scene at Graham's. Before service, as in all the restaurants in which I've worked, it starts with prep, and they have me prep a lot of vegetables. As I look around, I'm struck by the amount of product being broken down. Whole fish being skinned and filleted, giant cuts of meat, trimmed and portioned. This is all happening around me in an almost surgical setting. The breadth of skills these cooks are displaying immediately impresses me. I later find out, after talking to some of the team, they all have previously been chefs or *sous chefs* themselves.

A dish I had read about created by Graham, was *Foie Gras* Lollipops. After finishing my vegetable prep, a cook asks if I could help him make this very dish. I learn that Chef Bowles cooks the *foie* using a method, which also liquefies it. It is then placed into silicon molds and chilled. We unmold the semi spheres of *Foie Gras*, place them around a stick, and press until the two halves become one solid sphere. Then I rolled them in Cherry Pop Rocks candy, which clings to the *Foie Gras* sucker, and completes the dish. I begin to understand Graham's approach: Take a classic ingredient-pairing, and then put a unique and sometimes far out spin on it using nontraditional, fine-dining ingredients. I pick up on the riff immediately, being a lover of *foie*. Pop Rocks fills in for the usual fruit-based sweet element which almost accompanies it.

Then, before long, they have me cooking. I make a wonderful roasted red pepper and red onion and brown sugar coulis for the lamb dish. I start by tossing ten red peppers and four red onions in a bowl with olive oil, salt and black pepper. I then place them on a sheet pan and generously toss brown sugar over the peppers and onions. I put them into a hot oven, around 400 degrees and let them roast until they start to char, about fifteen minutes.

I then pulled them out and removed the stem and seeds from the red peppers. I put everything into a blender added a little water and blend it until it turns into a thick paste. I add a little more water, maybe a quarter of a cup, turn the blender on again, and let it go until it forms a nice puree. I give the blend to the guy at the grill, who needs it for his dish. Before long other cooks are giving me tasks for their stations, teaching me at times how to prep a specific component. I learn some cutting edge micro-gastronomy techniques; whatever they want, I gladly do.

One thing I notice during this tour of superstar kitchens is that the restaurants share many techniques and approaches. One technique is known as *sous-vide* – French for "under vacuum" – which involves cooking product in airtight plastic bags in a water bath at a low temperature. Many top chefs use this technique, albeit in different sequences, with different marinades and different effects. Graham Elliot's Buffalo style Chicken is my first experience of prepping and cooking a sous-vide prepared dish.

I start by skinning and deboning chicken thighs. I then roll them up into tight bundles, and wrapped each one in plastic wrap. I put them in the immersion circulator hot water bath, where they remain for several hours until they were needed for dinner service.

During service, I get on the hot line right away, which is fantastic, and I have no agenda other than wanting to help. I'm now assisting the hot appetizer station. "Fire a buffalo!" the chef commands.

I quickly unwrap the chicken thigh and drop it into the deep fryer. Next I grab a plate and squeeze decorative geometric lines of wing sauce on it. I add blue cheese and celery root slaw, hit the Budweiser emulsion with a stick blender in a nearby steel container, and put some Buffalo sauce in a bowl. Spinning around I pull the basket out of the fryer and grab the chicken thigh still covered in some boiling hot oil with my hand, and quickly put it into the bowl of Buffalo sauce. Using a slow up and down motion, the chicken, is quickly coated in sauce, and I place it onto the celery root slaw on the plate. I spoon some Budweiser foam over the top and hand the plate to Graham.

After inspecting it he gives me a quick smile and says "Great job, Boss." I find it kind of funny that Graham always addresses me as "Boss," but it goes a long way to making me feel part of his team, to be a great chef you need to be a team builder or your food will never be great; after all it's the team doing the cooking. His positive energy and passion for food is always omnipresent in his kitchen. I'm happy to be line cooking again, and now with a great chef – the polar opposite of the unhappy Chef Harry.

Throughout the evening, I kind of roam and help whatever station needs help. They've got three *sous chefs,* all coming with Graham from Avenues, one *Garde Manger*, and one pastry chef; and on the hot line they've got a guy on fish, a guy on meat, a guy on hot appetizers, and a guy on a station making edible cocktails. And I am talking serious cooking going on here. If there's a lamb dish being offered, these guys are butchering their own lamb legs. There are no prep cooks, saucier, or butchers here. Each cook is responsible for each and every component of every dish at their station. It requires lots of skills, and very long hours, even by professional kitchen standards. And when it gets busy, the rhythm is smooth and efficient. Nobody's yelling or whining or causing a scene. Certainly no count-downs. Graham is expediting the orders himself, so the sequencing is letter perfect.

It is a pure pleasure to be working at a place with this level of craft, making the components to extremely creative dishes such as the Gnocchi with Grilled Asparagus, Fried Egg and Truffle Oil, and Risotto with Braised Onion, Green Apple, Wisconsin bacon, and Cheeze-its, the Prime Pork Rib Chop with Grits, Collard Greens, Watermelon Chutney, and Root Beer Barbecue Sauce; and the Pistachio Crusted Lamb with Israeli Cous Cous, Shaved Fennel, Kalamata olive, and Red Pepper Coulis.

Which is another benefit of doing a *stage*: They feed you. And the food at Graham Elliot's is just phenomenal. Chef Graham hands me my supper, Wild Skate sautéed in Brown Butter, served on top of a crispy Polenta cake, Swiss Chard, and topped with a Caper Chutney. A dish I was eyeballing all night, as I was making Hot Apps next to the fish guy. At the end of my first day, Graham is pleased enough with my skills and attitude and work ethic as a line cook to ask me to come back. I gladly accept his offer, and agree to come back the following Tuesday...

...after I get a taste of working with another superstar: Chef Martial Noguier.

Friday, I go over to one sixtyblue and check in with the front person. I tell them I'm here to work with the chef, and they summon the man. A minute later, out walks this dapper, charismatic, upbeat Frenchman in immaculate whites. I mean he looks like Jean Paul Belmondo in some lost art film, and he is such a great guy.

"Oh Wayne, I am *soooooo* happy you're here!" He actually puts his arm around me. "Let me show you around!"

He makes me feel at home immediately, and he gives me a grand tour. This is one of the finest chefs Chicago has to offer, and it feels — at least to me — that he's legitimately glad to see me, glad to have a former football-playing chicken cook from Skokie on board. The only problem is he can't find a chef jacket that fits me. I'm happy I brought my own.

The kitchen is open — my first — and it's huge. You do all your chopping and dicing and cutting and cooking and plating in full view of the diners, as though on stage, and the granite surfaces are buffed to a high-polished sheen.

It is spectacular, and now I'm meeting the crew, starting with the Chef de Cuisine, Greg Elliot, who is also a great guy, as are the cooks and the rest of the crew. But at one point, I'm shaking hands and meeting people, when we turn a corner and I see a familiar face.

Much to everyone's surprise, I say, "Hello Allison."

The young woman I worked with way back in the early days of the Hofbrau, the one I called Fiddlesticks, the one who was allegedly Chef Dan's girlfriend – she's standing in her whites in Martial's kitchen.

"Hi, Wayne."

She's not cold. Not exactly. She's not unfriendly. But I do note – over the space of a brief instant – a subtle hint of reticence in her voice. As though we shared a foxhole in some distant past war, and maybe she did some things that she was not exactly proud of, and maybe she doesn't want her new master to see that side of her.

The truth is, my Hofbrau days already seem to be fading in my memory. I am so beyond that place by this point. But I have no ill-will toward Fiddlesticks.

I'm on a new path now.

And that first day at one sixtyblue, I get another inside glimpse at a higher level of cooking. Martial immediately puts me on the hot line, cooking hot appetizers. The dishes are spectacular. For instance, these are just a few of the hot appetizers: Giant Sea Scallops on Jasmine Rice Pudding with Edamame, Thai Basil, and Coconut; Pan-fried Bobwhite Quail with Pate Negra Spanish Ham, grilled Radicchio, Candied Salsify, and Sassafras Glaze; Swan Farm Suckling Pig with White Asparagus Custard, Cracklings, Pea Shoots, and Alder Flower Syrup; and of course the ever popular *Foie Gras*.

I work the hot appetizer station that first day at One Sixty with a gangly, skinny kid from Kansas named Brian who's still got acne. The first thing he says to me is, "There's a guy working the *garde manger* station today. The guy's the biggest dick I ever met – don't talk to him."

And I'm thinking, *Yeah, well, maybe that guy's the second biggest dick since I'm talking to numero uno.*

But the most important thing about one sixtyblue is the simple, undeniable fact of the food: It is magnificent. And I really enjoy doing the work, prepping the best ingredients imaginable, making soups, bouillabaisse. They have this incredible dish – Green Garlic Soup* – which just blows me away. I'm trying to figure out how I can get a bucket of it to take home.

The pace is a little slower here, I'm noticing – very food focused – so it's very relaxing to work on the line. But like all lines, it has its moments of high-tension stress and personality conflicts. But on the whole, I am absolutely impressed.

At the end of that first night, Martial finds me and he asks me how I like working with his food.

"Fantastique!" I tell him.

---

* Sauté 1 cup of mirepoix with 1/2 teaspoon of kosher salt until soft, Add 1 quart of julienned green garlic (you can use the entire green stalk), sauté until the garlic softens, deglaze with 1/2 cup of white wine, add a bouquet garnie (1 sprig of thyme, 4 peppercorns, 1 bay leaf, 1 sprig of parsley, all wrapped and tied in cheese cloth,) cover with chicken stock. Simmer for 20 minutes and check seasoning. Transfer to a blender and add 1/2 cup of boiled potatoes (optional) and 1/4 cup of cream. Puree until smooth, and taste for seasoning. You can strain it through a fine sieve for a smoother soup.

He asks if I'm ready to come to work for him now. He reminds me that it may very well be months before Tony opens.

"Martial," I say, "you don't even know if I can really cook. I didn't do that much tonight."

He looks at me with that chiseled French movie star face and purrs: "I can tell you have ze *passssssssion!*"

Again how can I refuse? I tell him I'll come back again the next day…

…and I do, and I spend another night sautéing on the hot appetizer station, and I'm getting better and faster, and cooking more and more fabulous dishes.

One thing I notice during this tour of superstar kitchens is that the restaurants share many techniques and approaches, such as *sous-vide.* Other techniques I'm seeing at both places: *Foams*, which involve mixing natural juices and sauces with an emulsifying agent such as lecithin, and then whipping the product into a light, airy froth; *gelees*, which are a sort of upscale gelatin; *faux caviars*, which involve a chemical process of turning food items such as soy or tapioca into beautiful pearls of different colors and flavors; and last but not least, the *"slow cooked egg."*

This is a staple of molecular-gastronomy, and one sixtyblue makes good use of it. The process involves cooking an egg in an immersion circulator, which is a big water bath device that keeps the water at a constant low heat, around 135 degrees, and circulates the water around the product. You cook the egg for forty-five minutes. The result is a very soft, creamy egg – fully cooked, almost like a poached egg, but more stable – and you can taste the difference.

But as the days pass, and I keep alternating between the two places, I start to lean toward one sixtyblue as a temporary home.

With each shift, I'm cooking more and more dishes at Martial's place. As I arrive early one day I see Martial prepping a huge lobe of Foie Gras. "Bonjour, Chef, are we serving Foie tonight?"

"Yes, it is going to be a special appetizer from your station," he responds without looking up from the delicate butchering process. He then carefully slices and weighs each portion.

During service he comes over to my station, which is hot appetizers. We have an order for the special, and the chef wants to show us the correct way to cook it. The Foie sizzles as it hits a hot pan, in a second pan go rhubarb sticks, ginger and lemon confit, heated in a simple-syrup of sugar dissolved in an equal amount of boiling water. The *Foie* sears in its rich rendered fat for a short time on both sides, and then plated in the center of the dish, the rhubarb and sauce are artfully put on and around the Foie. Mache greens are placed on the side, and then the surprising finishing touch…freeze dried strawberries are strewn around the Foie. The plate looks like edible art.

I continue to be wowed by both of these superstar chefs, discovering the surprising similarities in ingredients and modern techniques, but resulting in two entirely different types of cuisine of Graham and Martial. I'm beginning to understand the conceptual approaches, which make up the basis of their fantastic food.

At one sixtyblue I end up working the grill/sauté station there with the *Chef de Cuisine*, Greg Elliott. Now I'm really spinning out some great dishes, such as the Le Quebecoise Veal Tenderloin with Kohlrabi-Vanilla Puree, Hon Shimeji Mushroom, Fried Gnocchi and Chamomile. Since the pace is slower here, I can really concentrate on the techniques and the cuisine and the personality of Martial's food. Martial is such a positive influence on everybody in his kitchen – everybody loves him, and more importantly, everybody *respects* him. Martial is living proof that being a great cook and getting respect does not have to come from fear or subservience or hate.

I will go as far as saying you can taste it in Martial's food.

It's in the rich, deep notes of the slow-cooked lamb loin, and it's in the lushness of the prime Delmonico steak. And it's present in the spectacular and yet simple French comfort food known as the *Pomme Puree*. First developed by the world-famous Chef Joel Robuchon, this ain't your father's mashed potatoes. The *pomme puree** served at One Sixty consists of Yukon Gold potatoes, and the rest is – you guessed it – butter and cream, the twin diet-busting muses of upscale restaurants everywhere. I'll say it again: You cannot have too much butter in a dish. You

---

* 1 pound of butter and 2 cups of warm cream for 10 large Yukon Gold potatoes (about 4 lb.) Russet potatoes also work well. Start potatoes in cold water. Stir with a spatula if you don't have a food mill or a Kitchen Aide with a paddle.

simply cannot do it. If you want to lose weight, skip over this part.

It is a thrill for me during this time at One Sixty to finally make this indescribably delicious side. The potatoes are peeled and boiled first, which is the condition they're in when I get them, and then I add butter and put them through a food mill. Then I add salt and put the mixture in a big stainless steel bowl and take the bowl over to the mixer and hit it with the paddle. While it's mixing, I slowly add warm cream. And then the potatoes go through a "tami" – which is a fine mesh wire strainer – which yields an absolutely smooth product with nary a lump in sight.

You would think this would be good enough. Oh no. Just wait. We keep the mixture warm in a *bain marie* - hot water bath until an order comes up. And then to finish it off, we whip some heavy cream and fold *that* into the warm puree, and add a dash of fresh thyme.

I will always think of the absolutely decadent lushness of this dish – in a word, happiness – whenever I think of working at one sixtyblue. In fact, the honest-to-God truth of it is, if I had never met Tony Priolo, and had not made that commitment, I would have certainly – unquestionably, without a doubt – stayed at one sixtyblue making these sensational dishes and working for the incomparable Martial Noguier.

But here's another thing that begins to happen during these hot summer days at One Sixty: I begin to see the light at the end of my journey.

I begin to sense the imminent arrival of a new Italian restaurant in town… a restaurant that will not only make a huge splash in a city already chock full of great Italian restaurants, but will also – ultimately – turn me into the line cook I always hoped to be.

PART FOUR

LITTLE DREAMS

"You have to dream before your dreams can come true."

\- Abdul Kalam

CHAPTER 18

If you time-traveled back to the 1970s – back to the days of Watergate and wide-ties – and you ended up in Chicago during the last gasps of the Daley political machine, you might run into a skinny, young Scilian-American boy named Tony Priolo. You might find him walking down a cracked sidewalk on the far northwest side of town, his Ernie Banks autographed baseball bat in tow. School's out for the summer, and there are baseball games to be played and vacant lots to be explored.

Little Tony's stomach is growling, though, because it's late in the afternoon, and he hasn't had anything to eat since he scarfed up two helpings of his Grandma's Faye's leftover veal at lunch. Now he smells something in the air that hooks him as sure as a fisherman's line snagging a salmon in Lake Michigan. It's a buttery, nutty, doughy smell hanging in the atmosphere, as sweet as spun sugar.

It's the aroma of cookies. Little Tony knows it well. It's coming from the cookie factory – just up ahead, on Harlem, not far from the Priolo house, next to the roller rink – and Tony makes a mad dash for the place. He finds the big brick building and goes inside the store.

The Maurice Lenell Cookie Company – launched back in 1937 by Swedish immigrants – is a Chicago landmark. Inside the store, wide-eyed kids like Tony can watch the conveyor belts through glass windows, the endless march of butter dough being formed, baked, and nestled into boxes, whirring to and fro like Santa's workshop. But the best part is when they give the neighborhood kids free samples of all the different flavors and styles of cookies, including Pinwheels, Chocolate Chip, Jelly Stars, and Almonettes.

Tony scores a handful of free cookies on that long ago summer day – and he trots out of the store and heads home with a smile on his face, gobbling the golden-brown, slightly flawed treasures. Little does the boy know, though, at that formative stage: Not only will he one day grow up to be a great chef, opening a new restaurant of his own design, not too far from this very spot, but he will also come so far full-circle in his life that he will one day befriend and actually hire *me* – the human Brinks Truck from the gridirons of Skokie – as a line cook...

...Wayne Cohen...

...the same guy who, as it turns out, had some success – enough to pursue a dream himself – as the president of that same Maurice Lenell Cookie Company, which stood for so many years on Harlem Avenue, tempting people with that trademark smell wafting over the rooftops.

Born in 1970 on the west side of Chicago, Anthony Priolo grew up on the hardscrabble streets of Norridge and Harwood Heights, going to Catholic schools, and living, if not exactly in abject poverty, in pretty meager circumstances. His father worked in construction – Tony's grandfather was a surveyor – so the Sicilian traditions of following in the family business were prevalent early on. But Tony was an active kid with a zeal for life. He fell in love with baseball at an early age. Wanted to be a pro. But he was also bitten with another bug that would shape his young life.

Like many immigrant families in the Windy City, the Priolo household enjoyed live-in grandparents, both born in Cimmina, Sicily, both assimilated by the great melting pot of Chicago. Italian was rarely spoken in the Priolo household, except for hushed tones during telephone calls. The old world was left behind. But Grandma Francis was a character, and a great cook. Once she was arrested – suspected of mob ties – for running numbers in a local restaurant. The fact that she was merely *betting* on the ponies, like everybody and their brother did in those days, was ignored by the cops. But this made little Tony worship the woman all the more.

He especially loved her cooking.

After grandpa died, Grandma Faye – who lived in the basement – babysat and regularly cooked for Tony and his sister and brother. Tony noticed the care and effort with which Grandma Faye shopped for meat at the local butcher. Meats were ground by hand. Trips were made all the way down to Little Italy in the South Loop to get the best cuts. Sausages were dried in the attic. This is the essence of rustic Italian cooking – the grandmother's birthright – to demand the very best ingredients. Faye was on a first-name basis with local green grocers and fishmongers, and she spent hours preparing family meals.

Tony started helping in the kitchen more and more. With the rest of the family working brutal hours to make ends meet, Tony ended up doing a lot of the cooking. Not only did he love executing Grandma Faye's old-school Sicilian cooking-style, he figured cooking was the smart way to go. Somebody else had to set the table, and somebody else had to clean up afterwards. By the time Grandma Faye passed away, in 1982, Tony was not only a pretty decent cook – adept at Sunday ragu, homemade cranberry pound cake, Veal Milanese, savory puff pastries, and kaleidoscopic Christmas cookies – he had also decided he wanted to be a professional chef.

Grandma Faye left a small, tin file-box of recipes behind, a loving artifact, which Tony Priolo still possesses to this day. The tin box is a symbol of many things. It is a symbol of the oral history passed down in Italian families. It is a symbol of a cuisine originating out of poverty, a food that comes from the humble need to stretch resources – a single hog, a small garden, a cheap basket of corn meal – with panache and style and, above all else, flavor.

The little tin file box also represents love.

For Italians, food is often the way love is expressed. Opening oysters on Chistmas eve with mom and pop. Fishing for smelt in Lake Michigan. Picking wild cardoons down by the brickyards with sis. These memories are what imprinted Tony Priolo at an early age – they got "in his blood" – and they formed a lifelong love of cooking.

And this love – manifested by passion, perfectionism, and purpose – carried through every milestone of Tony's subsequent development as a professional chef.

After graduating from high school, Tony Priolo goes directly to the Cooking and Hospitality Institute of Chicago to learn the profession from the ground up. He starts getting jobs immediately. He works at a restaurant called Le Plume and learns the French fundamentals. He works at other French places and excels, and eventually becomes a top *sous chef*, but something is missing.

He feels it in his heart, in his gut. He has to go back to his first love, his passion, the family tradition, the cuisine which is still in his blood, as strong as ever. He takes a cut in pay to work at Il Toscanaccio, a Tuscan trattoria-style restaurant owned by the famous restauranteur Pino Luongo. Renamed Coco Pazzo Café a few years later, the place is perfect for Tony – a casual Tuscan café that serves meticulously prepared and yet simple cuisine.

Within months, Tony proves himself one of the most valuable players in the Coco Pazzo organization. His exacting approach – combined with his bone-deep love and understanding of Italian food – send him up the corporate ladder. He becomes executive c chef at the flagship restaurant on Hubbard Street, and eventually becomes partner. He is there for eleven years, maintaining unprecedented consistency and excellence, and also building one of the great kitchen crews ever assembled for a fine Italian dining establishment.

By this time, I had become... well... I guess you could say I had become a regular at Coco Pazzo. I just love the food, and I discover that this soft-spoken chef – who looks a little bit like Michael Imperioli, the young actor who plays Christopher on *The Sopranos* – is just about as friendly a sort as you're ever going to meet.

We start hanging out after busy services, talking Italian and French food, and just basically sharing our mutual passion. I certainly have no idea, during those late night kibbutzes, that a series of events are about to bring us together. If you told me that Tony would one day give me the opportunity to fulfill my *own* lifelong dream, I would have said you've had one too many Sambucas.

It starts with another feeling deep within Tony that something is missing. He has always harbored the goal of one day opening his own place, and now, as he closes in on over a decade of service to Coco Pazzo, he decides to pull the trigger on one last important dream.

Piccolo Sogno.

Italian for "Little Dream."

Tony drives by the perfect property one day, at the corner of Halsted and Grand, and the wheels kick into motion. Tony calls his dear friend – the former General Manager at Coco Pazzo Cafe, and future partner, Ciro Longobardo – and tells him he has found the future home of their baby, Piccolo Sogno. Ciro gets on the phone immediately and starts the process of securing the property and signing a lease.

A native of Naples, a graduate of the renowned Hoteliere School in Italy, and trained in Switzerland, Ciro Longobardo is a compact, stocky, well-groomed man with a preternatural nose for wine. He has designed wine lists for some of the top restaurants and hotels in Europe, and has become a consultant for U.S. importers. Ciro will become an enormous part of this little dream, and its unique approach to fine yet simple Italian dining.

As the months pass, Tony begins to put brick and mortar to his dream.

The build-out transforms a run-of-the-mill space into a austere, clean *art galleria* you might find in Venice. Terrazzo floors, Venetian plaster walls, marble bar, Italian artwork on the walls, and chandeliers from the famous glass-making island of Murano, all give the place a quiet authenticity you rarely find in this city. Exposed brick, an outdoor *piazza* under a canopy of white birch, and an open kitchen with a prominently visible wood-burning oven add a rustic tone to the atmosphere and also capture the feel of the culinary philosophy that started way back with Grandma Faye: *To get at the heart of simple Italian food, prepared by hand with local ingredients and served with local wines.*

The last piece of the puzzle is the crew. Because of non-compete clauses in Tony's contract, he'll have to build a new crew from the ground up. He knows everybody in this town, though, and he can leverage eleven years of good vibes and favors and advice he has handed out like so many First Holy Communion Cards.

This is where I come in.

After Tony makes me the offer I wouldn't dream of refusing, I feel like I'm training for a milestone moment in my *own* life – my own "little dream," as it were.

It is July now, and I've been cooking professionally for exactly one year. But it's a year that feels like ten. Probably because of all that I have learned, all the characters with whom I've been dealing, all the misadventures and unexpected slams and personal victories. I've learned so much, but I've learned on the job, always with the understanding in the back of my mind that it's all sort of transitory and for-educational-purposes-only.

Now I'm about to make a commitment. It goes unspoken between me and Tony, for the most part. But as "orientation day" at the restaurant approaches, I'm starting to realize I'm truly entering a new era in my life as a professional cook.

Everybody's there. Servers, managers, bus boys, dishwashers, prep cooks, butchers, the whole family tree. It's like going to a party without being sure you know anybody, and suddenly you see all these familiar faces. I see Ciro, whom I know from the days he first started at Coco Pazzo, years ago, and I also know some of the waiters from the better restaurants around town. I know one of the other cooks, Chava, with whom I worked at one sixtyblue. "What are you doing here?" Chava says, and I laugh. I think everybody's still trying to figure out this fifty-two year old line cook with the linebacker's build and mysterious back-story. But it's exciting, and it also has that bright and shiny first-day-of-school feel to it.

Over the next few days we do some private cocktail parties and have a soft opening to get on our feet, and business is instantly brisk, and I begin to learn how a new place comes together in Tony's world.

The publicity is like nothing I've ever seen. We're in all the major newspapers, we're in *Chicago Magazine*, we're in all the blogs, we're in Yelp, Metromix, Chow Hound, you name it. Tony is a well-known chef, and there is a major buzz. Everybody's pumped. And I'm ready to rock and roll.

Being a top flight Italian restaurant, the "Line" at Piccolo is set up differently than those of the other restaurants I've worked. There is one guy on Pizza at the wood burning oven, two on the Pasta station, myself and one other on Sauté'/Grill, and two people on Garde Mange'/Dessert.

Like every kitchen, it starts with the prep list, and the prep list starts with cutting vegetables. No matter how glamorous the surroundings, no matter how sexy the setting, it always starts with cutting vegetables. But I'm doing it now in this fabulous, gleaming new open-kitchen, and I'm getting to know the essentials of the Italian mise en place. I'm cutting zucchini, peppers, eggplant and onions for the companata, and I'm working with stuff like rapini (broccoli rabe), semolina, polenta, farro, basil, fregola, veal demi glace, rosemary, sage, squash blossoms, capers, and fennel fronds. I'm madly making notes, and I'm really jazzed because I'm getting to the point where I feel like I don't have to write stuff down as much anymore.

You get to that point where you just know what you're doing.

This is not to say you're perfect. You'll never be perfect.

For example: One of the first shifts at Piccolo Sogno, I'm slicing grape tomatoes in that clean, new chamber of terracotta tile, and feeling really good about myself, focused on the task at hand, and soaking in all the excitement buzzing around me, when I sense a presence standing next to me.

I turn and look into the placid, controlled face of Tony Priolo. He looks at me with a smile. "F-Y-I, Wayne," he says very softly. "You should be done with that by now."

"Yes, Chef." I hear him loud and clear. But this is classic Tony Priolo. He is, in many ways, the dream chef (no pun intended). He's not a screamer, he's not a bully, he's not histrionic or mean or melodramatic; he's simply a perfectionist. And he rules his roost with a fusillade of quiet — sometimes stinging – comments. Adjustments. Nudges. Zingers. Which can sometimes cut you worse than any knife.

On another occasion, during a crazy rush early in the restaurant's life, I'm cooking like crazy. I'm exhilarated, and I think I'm doing the job. But the truth is, I'm still the junior guy, and I'm feeling my way through the system. To make matters more interesting, we are constantly being slammed, so I have little time to ease myself into the system. In fact, we have been slammed from the moment we softly opened the doors. It is just relentless.

On top of this fact, I'm still trying to understand the lingo and the hybrid Spanish/Italian that comes roaring at me on the line. "Segueway," I hear in heavily accented voices. "Ordering Two Angello! Four Salmone! Three Battuta!"

I echo back at them (so they know I heard): "Two Angello, four Salmone, three Battuta!"

A moment later: "Fire! Two Fritura! Fire! Two Fiore! Fire! Three Angello! One Tonno!"

"Fire two Fritura, two Fiore, three Angello, one Tonno!"

My head is spinning, but I'm keeping up with it through sheer force of will.

And that's when I hear Tony's voice calling out: "Hey Wayne!"

I look up from my acres of food. "Yes, Chef?"

"It's not so glamorous, is it?" He grins, and I laugh and shake my head...

...but what I'm really thinking to myself is this: *It is pretty glamorous to me.*

But that's Tony at his thorniest. He keeps things from boiling over with humor – sometimes gallows humor, sometimes sarcasm – which breaks the tension and, most importantly, keeps the machine running, humming along. He is a *mensch* but he also knows what he wants at all times, and his eyes are everywhere all at once.

And his instrument – his Stradivarius – is his crew.

I get to know the names before I learn the personalities and quirks. The two guys on pasta: Carlos and Gabriel. On pizzas: Ishmael. On *garde manger*: Graziella and Chava. The Chef de Cuisine is one of the nicest, warmest guys I've ever met in this business: Marcello. And I'm the grill man. Not only am I – by far – the oldest cook, but I'm also the only Gringo. And I'm as happy as I've ever been in a kitchen – doing what I've always wanted to do: cooking on the hot line beside one of the best crews in the city in a fantastic restaurant.

The grill at Piccolo is a wood-burning rig, beautifully made, and my first. Tony shows me how to operate it, how to load the wood and lump charcoal. My responsibilities include making the hot appetizers; working the fryers for various breaded delicacies; grilling meats such as whole Polletto (baby spring chicken), Angello (t-bone lamb chops), Battuta (double chicken breasts), Salmon, and Tuna filets; grilling vegetables, and grilling seafood such as Calamari, Octopus, and Shrimp. I'm also doing the hot appetizers on the fly. By design. For instance, I'm learning how to keep a ton of stuff going at different cook times on the grill, while simultaneously doing the ancillary stuff like breading calamari and frying them to order. Also, there's a tremendous amount of stopping, shifting, and readjusting. It takes me a while to get used to it.

Another challenge, which takes me a while to acclimate myself to, is the Italian system of ordering. There are no tickets. An order, which comes in off the printer, is referred to as a "*segueway*." A "fire" is a "*via*." And in Tony's world, a "fire" means you have seven minutes. That dish better be heading out the window at 06:59 or before, or you will live with the fishes. "*Via! Via! Via!*" the expo is yelling with his thick accent, and again, here come these orders for elaborate Italian dishes – and the names are often like music – being shouted out in Spanish.

It takes me a while to re-tune my ears.

But this is what I wanted. This is the challenge. And the fact that the business that first week is unexpectedly heavy is not something Tony really expected. But I don't mind. I'm prepared for some major "contact-sport" cooking. It's like playing in the Super Bowl with a team of outstanding athletes, and I am really starting to feel like a top line cook, like I belong.

But there's one more key member of this All Star Team I have yet to mention.

In many ways he's the epitome of what being a cook is all about.

He's the Chef of Tomorrow, and in some ways a perfect symbol of Tony's genius with people.

CHAPTER 19

Born in Guadalajara, Mexico, in 1979, Miguel Solorio grew up in a large family. He was a big kid, sturdy, but with a kind, eternally boyish face. He was also drawn to Italian cuisine at an early age. His grandfather was a Spaniard, and little Miguel often shopped with the old man at the local Italian market, getting things like prosciutto and fresh mozzarella. Guadalajara is an international city, and Miguel soaked up the influences.

At twenty-four years of age, Miguel emigrated to the United States to find steadier paychecks and bluer skies.

He initially landed in Chicago and nabbed a job as dishwasher at an infamous west side hang-out called the Twisted Spoke. Part yuppie bar, part biker tavern, part hipster eatery, the Spoke serves pretty decent Mexican/American grub disguised by special events like "Whiskey Wednesday" and "Smut and Eggs Saturday," the latter a neighborhood favorite, during which porn films are screened and accompanied by items from the Biker Brunch menu.

Miguel started venturing into the Spoke's kitchen, and started learning the craft of cooking. From there he worked at a few pizzerias and a few upscale places, and eventually landed at Coco Pazzo, where he met his future mentor and boss, Chef Anthony Priolo. Miguel was natural with the cuisine. He had a passion for cooking – especially Italian food – which immediately caught Tony's attention.

Plus Miguel Solorio also showed an ineffable combination of traits that truly put him at the top of the pyramid: He had a great "eye" for plating and presentation; he was relentlessly hard-working; and he had a very even-keeled manner. This combination is as rare in the restaurant world as albino tigers.

Over time, Miguel Solorio rose up the ranks of the kitchen brigade at Coco Pazzo, and soon was one of the top line cooks there. When word began to spread that Tony was thinking about opening his own place, Miguel started dreaming of maybe following the good-natured maestro. Tony was thinking the same thing. And eventually Miguel was offered a job as line cook at Tony's new place. This was a huge step for Miguel, professionally, personally, spiritually. His reputation would be on the line. His life would never be the same.

I love working with Miguel. He's a big bear of a young man with a huge heart and lot of patience, and he's a top-top-*top* line cook – my partner on the Grill/Sauté station, eventually elevated to *sous chef* by Tony. In fact, I instantly bond with Miguel when

I learn that he, too, worked at one sixtyblue for a while. I find out that we both have this huge regard for Martial, and I even find out that Martial always wanted Miguel to stay and work for him.

My common experience immediately gives me props and credibility with Miguel.

Over that first week, getting slammed every night, I work the grill – with Miguel on sauté – and I get to know the man very quickly. It's just me and Miguel, and the chemistry between us is great. We really develop a tremendous rapport in the midst of this constant rush. Miguel is steady, level-headed, strong, and precise.

Miguel Solorio is the perfect quarterback for this team. No matter how slammed we get, the big man stays cool and focused on the seven-minute clock. He's like a machine. He doesn't get rattled, he doesn't get mad, he is simply relentless about quality and speed. That is the essence of greatness in the world of high-volume fine-dining – quality and speed.

For example, one day, while doing an order/fire, which involves sausages, which is just one of the dishes on the ticket, Miguel looks at me and says, "Wayne, how long for the sausages?"

I go, "Five minutes."

Five minutes later – to the second – he looks at me and says, "Wayne, where are those sausages?"

"Two minutes, Miguel."

He glances at me very briefly, without emotion, without judgment, and says, "Wayne, you told me five minutes ago that the sausages would be done – and it's been five minutes – so they're done."

"Okay, Miguel, they're done." I'm thinking, *Maybe if I wave my hand over them they'll magically be done*, but instead I cut them on the bias, and then *boom*, I flash them in the salamander, then plate them on top of the braised cannellini beans* and rappini; and out they go.

•   •   •

"Wayne, I'm sorry." Tony is wiping his hands in a towel after a busy night, talking to me as the crew cleans and shuts the place down. "I never expected this."

What he's talking about is the volume, the level of business we're doing right out of the gate. We're doing two hundred and seventy people on a Tuesday night. We're doing two-fifty on a Sunday between 5:30 and 7:30, and we are short-handed. Tony had planned to work alongside me during those early weeks, help me get my Italian legs; get me oriented to their system. And he tried. He would come over during a dinner rush and show me stuff like the best way to use a spatula on a fish or

---

* Heat up 1/4 cup of Olive Oil in a pot, add 1 clove of garlic sliced thin and chopped Rosemary from two sprigs. Cook for 30 seconds, add 1 quart of cooked cannellini beans and 1/2 teaspoon of salt, cook stirring for about a minute, add 1 cup of white wine and reduce by 2/3. Add 2 cups of chicken stock to cover, and 1/3 cup of Tomato Sauce, season with salt. Stir until most of the liquid is almost gone and beans are tender.

the best way to keep a sauce going. But then he would have to supervise another rush because he is a micromanager, and he's expo-ing everything himself. The thing about Tony Priolo is, he loves his work, and unlike a lot of other chefs, he is, and continues to be, a great line cook. He gets a huge charge out of working the line. And because of this, he's a little tense about his line cooks performing at their peak.

"I thought we would have a lot more time for me to work with you," he says.

"I'm good, Tony. I'm getting my rhythm, and we're really putting out great food."

Tony agrees, and he says he'll try to spend more quality time with me on the line. I thank him. And it's all good – except for this nagging little feeling in the pit of my stomach that the pressure is starting to get to me just a little bit. It's ironic that I would get nervous for the first time in my career, not in the kitchen of an unbearable chef like Lovable Harry at *Mon Oncle Gaston,* but in the presence of a guy I admire so much and enjoy cooking for.

I think it's because I care so much about Tony's restaurant. This is *it* for Tony. This venture is *just* Tony and his partner Ciro. If this place – God forbid – goes down in flames, so does Tony. And I really – really – want Tony to succeed. Which is why, one day, I'm plating an order of Calamari and sensing that Tony's hovering. And I'm focusing on getting the deep-fried delicacy plated perfectly....

"Are you nervous?" Tony asks. It's not a snide comment. He's genuinely interested. Like a scientist observing a natural phenomenon in his laboratory.

I look down at my hand. It's shaking. "No, Tony, I'm not really nervous," I tell him, looking at my hand, which is shaking like it belongs to somebody else. "At least I don't feel nervous."

Later I realize that it's not exactly nerves. It's about *caring* so much. It's about me caring because *Tony* cares so much. And I'm sure I'm not the only guy shaking. On the eighth night of torrential business, for example, the entire kitchen is deluged with orders, and mistakes are being made, and the POS system is going haywire, and new servers are screwing up orders, and finally Tony stares straight ahead and announces to nobody in particular, more to the whole universe: "This is the worst night of my life."

By the second week on the grill, I'm getting the system down pretty well, and the restaurant is finally hitting its stride (while continually being slammed every night). We're getting rave reviews, and I'm paying close attention to the press, because I don't want my dishes to be singled out as weak links. The consensus, though, is that Piccolo Sogno is the new star on the block. Chicago is many things, but one thing is undeniable: It is an Italian restaurant town.

And Piccolo Sogno is the big leagues of fine Italian dining. The *sous chef* from the renowned Gene and Georgetti is the butcher for the place. The olive oil and balsamic vinegar are custom made for Tony by artisans in Italy. Tony shows up every morning at 6:00 o'clock, baking the bread, making the gelatos, making everything in-house from scratch. He finally gets a pastry guy to take over some of the prep, but Tony is at the restaurant – *every single day* – from 6:00 in the morning to 1:00 the following morning. After a month, I tell him he needs to take a day off. "No," he says, very simply, very *matter-of-fact*, "I need to be here."

I'm working my tail off myself. I'm not as fast as I want to be, but Tony is telling me I'm doing great, and the other cooks are telling me I'm doing great, so who am I to argue? I'm also getting to the point at which I'm on intimate terms with the very specialized, very huge *mise en place*.

The "mise" here has a lot of the usual suspects you would find at any high-end place: the aromatic vegetables and oils and parsley and citrus. But now I'm working with Italio-centric stuff as well, stuff like Cecina (chick pea and rosemary fritters); Fiore (stuffed squash blossoms); rapini (broccoli rabe); arugula; Insalata di Pomidorini* (tomato-olive-and-basil salad); chopped rosemary and sage; pesto; rosemary; capers; paper thin garlic slices; grated Parmigiana Reggiano; Marsala wine; extra virgin

---

*Slice one pint of grape tomatoes in half, and place in a bowl, pit and chop 20 olives and add to the bowl with 1/2 cup of extra virgin olive oil, 1 tablespoon of sherry vinegar, and 2 tablespoons of chopped fresh basil. Stir and season with salt and pepper. Served as a topping sauce on grilled Salmon.

olive oil; aged balsamic vinegar. It's a beautiful Tuscan color palette governed by the seasons.

The third week, Tony moves me off the grill to pasta. I find it curious, especially considering the fact that I'm really getting to a good place at my station, mastering the cuisine. But he's the chef.

So I learn the pasta station. I really enjoy putting together simple delicious dishes. Like the handmade Malfatti with mushroom sauce. Malfatti is one of the myriad ingenious names the Italians have for pasta shapes. Literally meaning "broken or irregular," or "badly made," the Malfatti is anything but 'bad' – unless you mean "bad" in the hipster sense of *good-bad*, like *BAAAAHD*, man. Made from scratch every morning by Adrian, the pasta-maker, these little roughly-rolled marshmallow size pillows of spinach ricotta cheese dough can hold a multiplicity of sauces. The first one I make starts by hitting the hot sauté pan with oil then sliced garlic, next comes, mixed mushrooms (Cremini, Oyster, and Shitake), then porcini stock, chicken stock, rosemary, parsley, and butter. I then add the Malfatti and toss to coat with some grated Parmesano Reggiano, and plate. This is only one of the cornucopia of shapes and variants Tony puts on his wonderful seasonally-driven menus.

I take to the pasta station more than I even expected. I really enjoy prepping the vegetables and herbs, and sautéing all the various components and hitting the final product with just the right amount of spice or Parmesan cheese or pepper flakes, for just the right balance. And of course adding butter in the end to make the sauce silky and delicious. I enjoy the ballet of the two-man station, dropping the perfect portion of pasta in the water, cooking the noodles and gnocchi and marrying them to the just-made sauce, bringing the pasta dishes together.

And the station is really close to the front of the house, so everybody can watch.

It's an experience I only could have dreamt about on that day, so many months ago, when I staged at Coco Pazzo.

A few days later, Tony drops another bombshell on me in the middle of service. "We're gonna open up for lunch," he says, pacing back and forth in front of the pass, expediting orders. "Wayne, I want you to work lunches."

"No way," I say, unable to contain my disappointment. "I'm really digging working nights."

"Trust me, Wayne, it's for the best."

"Tony, come on, you know I'm not a morning person."

"No, it'll be good," he says, "it'll be good. You'll be able to work with me more."

"I don't know, Chef."

I go back to the grill station and continue cooking. And I'm thinking: *Not the ideal place for me.* I'm not really down with getting up early in the morning, and there's the rush hour drive to contend with, and I'm really enjoying being in the heat of dinner service. But then I think, *Who am I to be so choosy?* I do enjoy working with the prep guys in the morning, making all the sauces and the stocks, and these are really terrific guys. So I'll give it a shot. I made a commitment to Tony from the start, and if lunch is where he thinks I can best help his dream, I'll do my best.

The next day I come in and tell him I didn't mean to be argumentative.

I tell him I will do my best.

He says that's good enough for him.

The first week on the lunch shift, I drag myself out of bed at 6:00 in the morning, and I'm down at the restaurant by 7:00, and it's a grind. I'm really not digging it. Mornings, as I have said, just aren't my thing. But I'm doing my best, working alongside my new cohort, Felipe, and cooking great lunches. There's also a new pizza guy, Marcos, who is always singing, and who comes over at regular intervals to help me out at my station. Graziella has also switched to days, handling the pantry and desserts.

After six weeks, though, I am so exhausted by the new timetable, I decide to go to Tony and inform him that I might have to quit. I don't want to, but I made it clear that I wanted to work nights on the hot line. I was always clear about this. So one day, after service, I give Tony the bad news.

Tony looks at me and says, "You know what – let's try this: You don't have to come in at 7:00 in the morning. It's your station, you know what to do, and you're doing it. Come in whenever you want to."

I stare at him. "Seriously?"

He shrugs. "Just make sure you're ready for service. You know what you have to do. Let's try it this way for a couple of weeks... because I don't want to lose you."

CHAPTER 20

On the afternoon of my aborted resignation, I am so utterly blown away by Tony Priolo's commitment to *me*, I can hardly express my appreciation. But once again, this is precisely what makes him special.

So now it's *Theater du Tuscan Cuisine* every day at lunch, working the grill/sauté station, while the patrons watch like an audience at some *Verdi* opera. And I'm really digging it. Finally I'm one of those guys I've watched all my life in open kitchens. I've arrived.

And I'm getting into this new groove, and Tony's supervising, and he's very happy with the results. We're a precision drill team now. But that doesn't mean we're infallible.

One time – and this is when I'm back working a night shift, and it's slammed with three-hundred and eighty covers moving through the restaurant – we screw up on the number of *parpadelle* portions (which is a special that night) that we've got stored away in the low boys. A long, wide noodle, the *Pardadelle* with

225

Summer Vegetables are selling like the proverbial hot cakes. So I'm calmly working the station when I notice we're down to four portions left. So I alert everybody, including Tony: "Only four orders of parpadelle left, Chef."

"What?!" Tony says. "I made thirty! Check again!"

I do what he says, and I check the low-boy. But I know what I'm going to find. I'm not expecting more parpadelle to magically appear.

"Only four, Chef," I tell him again.

By this point, things are moving. Really moving. Tony is like an air-traffic controller, and dishes are circling the runway like rush hour at O'Hare. Hot trays of roasted whole fish from the wood-burning oven are literally being passed over my head by the pizza guy, and the heat is tremendous, but Tony is expediting everything, and dishes are moving quickly and professionally.

An order for two parpadelle comes in. I check the low boy and I look at Carlos. "Carlos, we only got one."

He looks at me like he's just seen a poltergeist leap out of the stockpot. "C'mon, c'mon."

"We only got one, Carlos. Tell the chef."

"No, I'm not telling him." At this point I can see into this man's soul, and I can see that same nervousness that I have felt.

"Tell the chef, Carlos."

"You tell the chef."

"Fine, whatever. I'll tell him." I shout to Tony. "Chef, we only got one order of Parpadelle left!"

"What?!" Tony gives us this truly amazed look, as though the earlier warning has completely slipped through the cracks of his memory, and now he's seeing a sign of the apocalypse, the rush swirling around him, everybody doing twelve things at once, the heat radiating like Death Valley. "Why didn't you tell me?" he says incredulously.

What can I say? We started with thirty orders, yes, and we sold twenty-nine, and there's nothing I can do about it, and now Tony is frowning like he's attempting to split the atom or tabulate the meaning of life. But then he does something that I will always remember, something that perfectly captures his essence as a chef.

Any other chef would simply go apologize to the patron, tell them we've run out, and unfortunately they'll have to order something else. Lovable Harry would most likely have one of his minions deliver the bad news. But not Tony Priolo. What does Tony Priolo do?

He drops everything, and he goes downstairs and makes another order of parpadelle. On the fly. From scratch. With his bare hands. Just like that. This is the reason I'm here, and the reason this place is buzzing with business.

Unfortunately, I have to go down to the cooler during this brief period to grab something, which necessitates me traveling through the prep area, while Tony is still down there, feverishly kneading dough. "You're killing me, Wayne," he says with a smirk. "You're killing me."

I let out a sigh. I could remind him that I told everybody we we're really low on parpadelle. I could also remind him that Carlos knew as well as I did that we only had one left. But those are the wrong answers.

The only correct answer for a line cook is what I said at the end of my long, weary sigh.

"I'm sorry about that, Chef."

• • •

Tongs and towel. Tongs and towel. Tongs and towel. This becomes second nature. Every surface is hellaciously hot in an Italian restaurant kitchen – in *any* good professional kitchen, for that matter – and you get so that the tongs and towel are an extension of your fingers. You're grabbing blistering-hot sauté pans with the towel, flipping stuff, turning stuff with the tongs, tasting with your finger, moving a pan to the speed table, readjusting seasonings, putting in your herbs, and flipping liquid into a sauce to loosen it. The only occasion you might use another tool is a large spoon to move sauces, or a spatula to flip items on the grill. But in terms of tongs-and-towel technique, Tony is the Maestro of the craft – he can move down the line with a towel and tongs, cooking with so much ambidexterity, so much multi-tasking finesse, you would think he was Giuseppi Verdi conducting *Rigoletto*.

The weeks of working the lunch shift make me an even better cook. I'm now responsible for the Grill and Sauté stations by myself. As time passes I work with new people and new seasonal menus. One of them has several new dishes including Sformatto di Zucca*; a savory roasted squash flan plated with parmesan cream sauce, aged balsamic vinegar, and squash chips on top. Also added, La Ribollita Delfina; a thick Tuscan bread and vegetable soup, finished by sautéing it in a hot pan until a beautiful golden crust forms on each side. A dish Tony learned while cooking at the famous Da Delfina restaurant near Florence, Italy. Eventually I am responsible for preparing these dishes for the entire restaurant. The new menu also includes a beautiful Chicken Milanese. "Wayne makes the best Milanese I've ever tasted," Tony tells his managers one day during their daily lunch, much to my surprise and pride, a pleasant reminder of all the schnitzels pounded and cooked in the past.

I'm also learning how to sequence the components of a dish better: My favorite new dish is the Veal Scallopini Marsala, which is a sensational pan-seared veal dish with mixed wild mushrooms, roasted potatoes, and sautéed spinach, which I learn to sequence the Priolo way, potatoes first, always first, even before the veal, always the ingredient with the longest cook-time first. Tony also teaches me to finish your task first, and then go to what's "fired." Previously I was always dropping whatever I was doing when a new order was fired.

---

* Combine 1qt of squash roasted with a pinch of cinnamon, nutmeg, and allspice; and custard prepared by mixing 4 eggs and 2 cups of cream. Season with Kosher salt and pepper and pour into buttered ramekins. Bake at 400 degrees for a half hour or until hot and firm.

The truth is, I'm gaining more and more skills, which gives me more and more confidence. I'm getting to the point where I can rise to any challenge, no matter how arduous.

Like the time I have to dance around an oven guy during an unexpected lunch ticket.

On this particular day, at the end of the lunch rush, I serve the managers their traditional, laid-back, midday meal, and I'm letting the wood grill cool down, and turning off the burners. It's a few minutes after 2:00, and the oven repair guy shows up to work on my oven. The oven is part of my station, so this guy's got his tool box on the floor and his meter out, and his head is buried in the oven, which has been acting up lately, not getting hot enough. It's no big deal, though. I don't need to do much at the moment. The rush is over...

...that is, until the ticket printer starts rattling a little longer than usual. Felipe, my partner in the kitchen that day reads it. "Oooohhhh shit," he laughs as he glances back over his shoulder at me, and hands me the ticket at 2:40. "It's all you, Wayne!" His laughter echoes on his way out of the kitchen as he vanishes into the afternoon. Tony's gone; Miguel's not around; and Felipe has just vanished (he has a second job – which he has to be at by 3:00 each afternoon).

Now I'm the only one working the kitchen and I've only got a couple of burners going. The rest of the burners are occupied by giant stockpots of ragus and sauces reducing. Plus, the oven guy is still there, futzing with the oven. And now I got this big ticket: A couple of orders of sausages and beans, two Griglia Mista's (wood-grilled calamari, shrimp and octopus), and one Vitello Scaloppini Marsala.

I've been through this before. I have almost two years of battles behind me. I have that first slam night at the Hofbrau, when I did almost eighty pick-ups by myself, I have the infamous Oktoberfest slam, and the Sonja solo night at Mon Oncle Gaston. I have all the battle scars like faint tattoos on my hands and arms – the burns and cuts of a pro, the ghosts of old skirmishes with hot handles – and most importantly I have the Tony Priolo system...

...which is why I waste no time getting the pans down on the flames, getting the roasted potatoes going first, hitting them with rosemary, sage and parsley, and then the beans – Tony's axiom ringing in my ears, the longest cook times first, always first – and then I get another pan roaring hot, because a pan has to be extremely hot to put the right sear on the Veal, and I get the sausages on the wood burning grill, and then I hurry over to the low boys for the *Griglia Mista* seafood, swerving around the oven man, grabbing seafood to season, coming back around the oven man, and then throwing shrimp, squid, calamari and octopus on the grill. Then I hit the roaring hot pan with oil and get the three pieces of veal down immediately before the whole range goes up in flames.

By this point, I'm in my element again, sweating profusely, enveloped in heat, grabbing a sizzle plate, taking the veal out of the pan, adding oil and mushrooms to pan the veal was in,

231

hitting it with chopped sage and rosemary, hitting it with the Marsala wine and some veal stock, then turning the sausage, checking the seafood, changing positions of stuff so it doesn't grill unevenly. Back around the protruding ass of the oven guy to the speed table for the arugula and potato wedges, then back around the oven guy to the burners, where I tend to the seafood, and I'm getting tired of dodging the repairman by this point, so I'm going down the line to other stations to finish my beans, and I'm using back burners, the heating singeing my arm hairs. I'm getting the rapini going in one pan, and I'm getting the spinach and garlic going in a second pan, and then back to the sausages. I finally get the oven-guy out of the way – the sausages have to finish in the oven – and I finish up the seafood.

By now it's plating time. So I get my plates down. I get the arugala and boiled potato wedges in a bowl, salt and pepper, lemon oil dressing, and then I plate the seafood. I put the lemon caper sauce on top of the seafood, and then I place the salad on top of that. And then I make sure the potatoes are nicely roasted, and they go up next, and then I put those up on the slide. I put the veal back in the pan with the reducing mushroom sauce, add a wad of butter, run down to the other station for the rapini and the spinach, add a little stock to the rapini, the cloud of fragrant steam rising like an atom blast in my face.

And finally I'm plating everything else, putting the beans in bowls, grabbing the rapini and putting it on top of the beans, then grabbing sausages and cutting them on a bias. *Oops.* Still a little pink. I flash them in the salamander, and then place them like flower petals on top of the rapini and beans. Potatoes and spinach down on the next plate. The three pieces of veal are shingled on the plate, and then I spoon the mushroom Marsala reduction over the veal. At last I grab my trusty squeeze bottle of extra virgin olive oil and I give the sausage dish that trademark rustic Tuscan flourish of a drizzled lariat of oil.

I glance at the clock, and I smile to myself, a pearl of sweat running down the bridge of my nose.

Nine minutes have elapsed since the ticket hit the POS system... not seven, but not bad.

Over the months, I get more and more comfortable at Piccolo. New folks pass through the system. Some stay, some go, but the vibe at Piccolo is always positive. Graziella, for example, is a tough, competent little gal, the *garde manger*, a star cook in her own right, happy to be working in a male-dominated pressure cooker. I'm feeling more and more like I fit into this little family. I'm coming in every morning now between 8:00 and 9:00, and everybody's greeting each other: *"Buenas Dias, Everybody!" I yell.* There's salsa music playing, and everybody is chatting as they work. Telling jokes. Cracking each other up. The mood is so upbeat at this place, and we're cooking at the highest level the whole time.

This is how a professional restaurant kitchen is supposed to run. This is how you translate raw labor and management into a dining experience.

What happens to me over the months of working at Tony's is not only a gradual deepening of my skills — I'm faster and better on the line than I have ever been – I also start to manifest the personality of the place: *"Buenas Dias, Senor! Buenas Dias!"*

I love cooking at this place – the same place every shift – and preparing the exact same delicious dishes, the same *mise en place*. This is at the core of great cooking. It is about replicating the same great food over and over and over. It is all about *this* plate, and then the next one, and the next one, meal after meal: And this discipline, this groove, suits me. I'm back where I started: Getting that Zen mindset, that blood-pressure lowering rhythm of each day.

I'm home.

I'm a hard-working line cook.

· · ·

A year can go by in the blink of an eye. And it can also contain a lifetime. I have been cooking at Piccolo Sogno for almost a year.

The bottom line for me – and for most professionals – is this: Despite the mind numbing repetition, and despite the back-breaking hours, and despite the paint-peeling heat, and despite all the little annoying impediments from management gaffs to petty in-fighting among immature staff... cooking on the line is a magnificent endeavor. If you have the discipline and you care about the food you're putting up on that pass, you can excel.

Over the course of this two year adventure — culminating with Tony Priolo's "Little Dream" — I have learned this about myself: This journey is more than a trivial, ego-driven thing. Sure, I wanted to see if I had what it takes to be one of those "guys-in-the-kitchen" whom I saw as a restaurant-goer. Sure, I wanted to challenge myself and see if I had the stones, skills and palate for it. But there has to be more.

What there has to be is passion: the sheer joy of preparing food. The sheer joy for cooking. You can call it love. Maybe love is better word. Tony Priolo taught me — and continues to teach me — this simple fact of life as a line cook.

You've got to love it.

And I genuinely do.

PART FIVE

SO YOU WANT TO BE A PRO

*"The difference between school and life? In school you're taught a
lesson and then given a test. In life, you're given a test
that teaches you a lesson."*

- Tom Bodett, *Humorist*

know what you're thinking. You're thinking, perhaps, just maybe... you could do this. Maybe you've got what it takes to be a pro, to stand the heat, to stay in the kitchen. After all, it ain't splitting atoms we're talking about here. Or maybe you're thinking: *No thanks, I'll just remain a foodie, I'll just continue tuning into Top Chef and cooking for my friends once in a while and leave it at that.*

No problem.

But if you're even remotely inspired by my story, and you have that fire in your belly for line cooking – and especially if you're thinking about going to culinary school – you might want to consider a few things before going out and buying that starched white chef jacket and funny hat (not to mention the exorbitant application fees).

Culinary schools have never been as popular as they are today. The National Center for Educational Statistics reports that the number of Americans getting bachelors degrees in the culinary arts has sky-rocketed – up thirty-five percent in 2006 compared to 2004. And nowadays, many culinary schools are as expensive as law school. For example, tuition at the Cordon Bleu in Paris for a fifteen-month program is $40,000. A two year associates degree at the local Culinary school can cost more.

Is culinary school necessary? You get a lot of different answers from a lot of different people in the industry. Many chefs believe it is an essential foundation from which to build (if you can afford it): You learn technique, you learn knife skills and food science.

But most industry insiders agree: It is decidedly *not* mandatory. Personally, every time I see a "So you want to be a chef" ad for culinary schools on TV, I can't help but chuckle.

I'll go even further. Cooking on the line is a purely a *hands on* craft — a skill that comes *only* from the scars and wisdom of surviving slams, thinking on your feet, *staying* on your feet for your entire shift, night after night after night. It is not something decoded in a textbook, or something spelled out on blackboards by scholars. In other words, you cannot *learn* it without *doing* it.

And the sooner you start doing it, the sooner you will learn it.

Hence we come to my dozen simple, easy to follow steps for becoming a pro without going to cooking school. Here they are, in no particular order:

1. Get Ready...............Get Ready.

First and foremost, you need to understand what great food and cooking is. You need to have that passion, and you need to be a great home cook. If don't think you're a great home cook, you're not ready; keep cooking at home. Most of you who are ready, you know who you are, and many of you know who you are *not*. You should know how to make a variety of sauces and dressings, you should know how not to burn a piece of meat, and know it's doneness by touch. This goes for fish and poultry as well. You also need to have your priorities straight: You're not going on this journey to get rich, to get laid, or to get famous. You're doing this because you love to cook, and you want to do it at the highest level on a daily basis. To put it another way, some musicians want to be composers or conductors – both of which are exclusive from playing an instrument – but other musicians get the maximum joy from simply playing the instrument. You should be the latter: You should simply want to cook... *professionally*.

2. Sharpen Your Skills.

Every time I walk into a restaurant kitchen for the fist time – with the goal of joining the team – it all starts with the knife, and vegetables. Know how to both julienne and dice. And know how to do it well. Always work as quickly and safely as possible. Onions, mushrooms, shallots, celery, and carrots, your first task and test in a professional kitchen is probably going to involve prepping some of these. Be prepared. Practice cutting these vegetables – both julienning, and dicing. Use the pinch grip to hold your knife: Hold your thumb and forefinger on the blade just in front of the bolster (where the blade meets the handle), pinching the blade, then wrap your other three fingers firmly around the handle. This is the grip of a professional. Grasp the vegetable with a "claw" grip, placing the product between your thumb and pinkie with your other three fingers on top. Curl all your fingers so your knuckles are the only part exposed. Using your knuckle as a guide, slice at a forty-five degree angle across your body. Practice slicing and dicing, first by cutting the onions in half through the root and stem ends. Then make precise 1/8" julienne lengthwise cuts. Go out and buy a bag of onions to practice on, and make onion soup or onion marmalade when you're finished. Next, practice slicing by keeping the tip of your knife on the board and rocking the blade in an up-and-down motion. This is particularly efficient on smaller vegetables.

Always place a damp towel under your cutting board, this will keep it from slipping, another professional trick.

Believe me, your knife skills will be the first thing you are judged on.

3. Sauté, Towels, and Tongs.

Also get used to the tongs-and-towel style of cooking. Consider everything – and I mean *everything* – to be hot in a professional kitchen. Grasp all hand-holds with the neatly folded towel. The steel tongs are self-explanatory and very inexpensive. Be able to grab scorching hot pans with your tongs, and maneuver them to burners. Practice using the tongs in both hands, because you often find yourself alternating hands when juggling pans and cooking.

It's also a good idea to practice your sauté pan skills. Know how to do the "flip," which is Basic Line Cooking 1-0-1 (lift the pan off the heat, thrust it outward until the food hits the curved edge, and then with a quick jerk of the wrist flip the food back to the center of the pan). Practice on dried peas or beans. Next practice sautéing vegetables. Finally move on to sauces.

4. Do Your Homework.

There are a great number of resources to sharpen your skills available from books and the internet. From sharpening knives to shucking oysters, it's all there for you to learn from, and much of it is free. *Cook's Illustrated* Magazine is a great resource for technique and food science. You can find instructional videos on Youtube, including many by chefs.

You might also want to read a book by Harold McGee called "On Food and Cooking: The Science and Lore of the Kitchen." This is the bible on all things gastronomic and scientific, and should be required reading for all serious cooks.

5. Look The Part.

When you go in for your internship or "stage," bring your own knives. They don't have to be expensive or made out of spun gold. They just have to be yours. At least an eight inch or ten inch chef knife, maybe a paring knife. Get them sharpened professionally – the sharper the knife, the safer the knife – or even better, get a hold of a sharpening stone and learn to do it yourself. Also learn how to "steel" your knife – which is not sharpening, but instead straightening the microscopic teeth on the cutting edge – because chefs watch this when they "audition" people. Go out and get a knife bag – they're only ten bucks. Get a pair of chef pants, and a chef's jacket. They're cheap and comfortable. Widely available on the internet. Modern Chef makes a great pair of inexpensive pants and jackets. Dark Cargo pants are also acceptable. Do not show up in jeans. Comfortable black shoes are best. Black clogs are standard in the industry. Make sure your shoes are clean. It's also good idea to bring your own headwear. Bakers caps or "skull caps" are the most common.

6. Be Prepared.

Always carry Band-Aids on your person. Simply stated: You're going to get cut and burned. And you don't want to have to run around, leaving the line, to look for a Band-Aid. I recommend Vitamin E lotion or gel caps (which you cut open to apply topically) and Bacetracin ointment for burns. Also have a Sharpie marker pen and a pocket notebook handy at all times. Sharpies are omnipresent in a professional kitchen, used constantly to record dates on masking tape, and just generally to label stuff. You also want to be able to take notes.

7. Know the Vocabulary.

Like every specialized industry, there's a lingo used by professional cooks and kitchen staff. As we've already discussed elsewhere in the book, "Yes, Chef" is the universal response. Good manners are the coin of the realm. You cannot say "please" and "thank you" enough in a professional kitchen. Whenever you are near someone, you say "Behind!" ("Atras!" in Spanish). Everybody needs to know where everybody else is, especially with sharp tools, hot pots and pans, and flames in action. "Hot!" or "Caliente!" are also very common interjections. When you're carrying your knife you say "Knife" or "Cochillo" or "Sharp!" Safety is the order of the day, everyday, and one of the skills you will be judged on. Needless to say, learning a little Spanish is invaluable.

8. Know Where IT Goes.

There are standard size containers to hold all the food stuffs. Most kitchen equipment is designed to accommodate these containers efficiently in your speed racks. A Hotel Pan is the largest of these rectangular containers, it is 12 X 20 inches, and there are also 1/2, 1/3, 1/6 and 1/9 pan sizes, 1/9 being the smallest. The depth ranges from 2" to 6". They are made from both plastic and stainless steel.

There are also plastic containers sometimes referred to as "Cambro's" or Lexan's of various sizes. They are usually marked with liquid measurements on their sides.

Deli's are plastic semi-see-thru cylinder containers, with lids. They come in one, two, and four cup sizes.

Sheet pans are large flat metal rectangles with very shallow sides. They come in two sizes full and half. Both have a small rim.

9. Work Clean.

This is another sign of a professional cook. Working clean means the consistent and repeated wiping and cleaning of your station. Make sure you're prepared to clean after every task. When you're done with each duty, your station should look like nothing happened there. Start doing this at home and make it habitual.

If you really want to impress a potential employer, consider going the extra mile and taking a food sanitation course and getting a Certified Food Manager license. These courses are offered by different organizations. Your local health department can provide contact information for you; and they are not that expensive, and only require a couple of days of your time.

10. Find Yourself a Job Cooking.

Start Hunting through Craig's List: (www.craigslist.org) This ubiquitous classified website, started in 1995 in San Francisco by Craig Newmark, has grown into the largest service of its kind in the world – with over 50 million monthly visitors. Right now, in most major metro areas, it is the prime source for job opportunities in the restaurant industry. Everybody from four-star fine-dining establishments to the neighborhood bar uses Craig's List to post job openings.

Network. Ask restaurant owners, managers, servers, and chefs you already know, about opportunities they are aware of. Anybody connected to a restaurant could hold the key to your career. The restaurant business is a very small world. All you have to do is ask.

There are opportunities to cook at Kitchens run by various charitable organizations. Volunteer and get experience. Work up the courage to walk-in to a restaurant's you like, and simply ask if there are any opportunities for a newbie. Also be prepared to work for free at first. Tell them you'll do a "stage" at their place. Who doesn't want free help? As I have been preaching, this is *di rigueur* in the restaurant world. Think of yourself as an actor auditioning for a part.

11. Be Part of a Team.

Respect. Respect. Respect. I cannot emphasize this enough. When you get on a line, introduce yourself to everybody, and defer to those who have gone before you. You can acquire a tremendous amount of techniques and knowledge from the other line cooks. Have a thick skin. Learn to take criticism. And don't show off or pretend to know something you don't. Always, always be on time. Most chefs are looking past superficial skills to something deeper and harder to define. Simply being a good worker with passion for food and a willingness to learn goes a long, long, long way with most chefs.

12. One Last Piece of Advice.

This last piece of advice has been floating around the restaurant business for years, and when I first heard it I thought it was so simple and yet so brilliant. In some ways, it sums up the subtext of this book and I offer it now with my good wishes for your future adventures Cooking On The Line:

KEEP YOUR EYES OPEN, YOUR HANDS MOVING, AND YOUR MOUTH SHUT.